Allô! Allô!

Ena Fowler

French role-play exercises to GCSE

HODDER AND STOUGHTON
LONDON   SYDNEY   AUCKLAND   TORONTO

Acknowledgements

The author is grateful to Nadine del Volgo and Lisette Rodrigues for their help and advice.

Illustrations by Stephen Fowler

British Library Cataloguing in Publication Data

ISBN 0 340 414820

First published 1988

Copyright © 1988 Ena Fowler

All rights reserved. No part of this publication may be reproduced or transmitted in any form or by any means, electronic, or mechanical, including photocopy, recording, or any information storage or retrieval system, without permission in writing from the publisher or under licence from the Copyright Licensing Agency Limited. Details of such licences (for reprographic reproduction) may be obtained from the Copyright Licensing Agency Limited, 33–34 Alfred Place, London WC1E 7DP.

Typeset by Gecko Ltd, Bicester, Oxon.
Printed in Great Britain for Hodder and Stoughton Educational, a division of Hodder and Stoughton Ltd, Mill Road, Dunton Green, Sevenoaks, Kent by Richard Clay Ltd, Bungay, Suffolk.

Contents

	Preface	4
1	Arriving at a campsite, youth hostel or hotel	5
2	Asking the way	17
3	Shopping	26
4	Travel by train, coach or plane	39
5	Arranging to meet someone	54
6	At a post office or bank, at the customs desk	59
7	At a cafe or restaurant	65
8	Lost property, repairs	73
9	Asking for information	79
10	Minor illness, injury, road accident, doctor	84
11	House and home	90
12	Places of entertainment	97
13	At a garage or petrol station	104
	Summary of useful phrases	109
	Aural questions for use with the cassette	110

Preface

"Allô! Allô!" has been written to give a thorough and enjoyable introduction to the oral section of the GCSE examination, with particular reference to the rôle-playing questions.

The chapters are topic-based, and the material within each is carefully graded so that there is work for each level of ability. In each chapter vocabularies and 'models' are given. If flashcards are made, containing pictures which represent the nouns in these 'models', the teacher can invent a good deal of extra classroom work.

There are many varied exercises, including some based on realia. The exercises are designed to elicit oral work at varying levels of difficulty. A particular feature of the book is the number of games suggested. These provide pair or group work and intensive use of the vocabulary.

The conversations at the end of each chapter have been designed to cover the requirements of the Boards' syllabuses, in full for basic (general) level students, and in part for higher (extended) level students. (It should be noted that Boards differ in their requirements for each level.)

The conversations are arranged in alternate lines of French and English so that each column is a self-contained testing unit, for use either in pair work or for a student on his/her own. A cassette of these conversations is available and provides a useful resource for pupils to work with either on their own or in groups. The cassette can also be used for aural comprehension; there are questions for this purpose at the back of the book.

Revision cards are also available to complement the book. There are fifteen different cards for each topic; the interviewer's script is on one side of the card, and the interviewee's instructions are on the other. In this way a class of thirty students can all do pair work on the same topic at once, passing round the cards to one another. I would suggest, by the way, that the students are urged to add 'monsieur', 'madame', 'mademoiselle' and 's'il vous plaît' wherever appropriate, even if there are no specific instructions about this on the cards as Boards may add marks for courtesies in the foreign language and deduct marks if they are missing.

It is hoped that by working through "Allô! Allô!" students will enjoy themselves, at all levels of achievement, and at the same time become able to cope orally with the basic situations of everyday life in France.

1 Arriving at a campsite, youth hostel or hotel

6 ALLÔ! ALLÔ!

Imagine that you are staying at the campsite on the previous page. Could you give directions to someone who didn't know his way around?

Examples:
1 Le terrain de volley est à gauche du tennis.
2 Le snack est à côté de la laverie.
3 Le tennis est à gauche de la discothèque.
4 Les tentes sont loin de la piscine.
5 Le terrain de pétanque est tout près du parking.

Here are the words that you will find most useful:

en face de	*opposite, facing*	à droite de	*on the right of*
à côté de	*next to*	à gauche de	*on the left of*
près de	*near*	loin de	*a long way from*
tout près de	*very near*		

You must also be clear about whether to use **du, de la, de l'** *or* **des**.
With the following words, use **de la**:

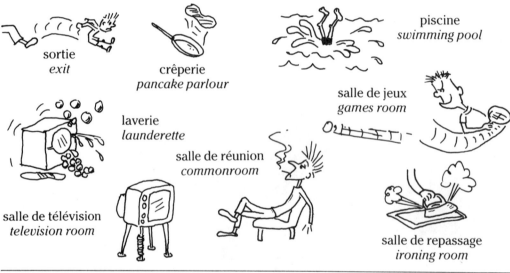

With the following words use **du**:

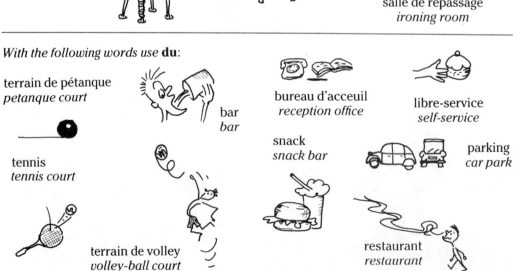

ARRIVING AT A CAMPSITE

With the following words, use **de l'**:

> de l'entrée *entrance*
> de l'aire de jeux pour les enfants *children's play area*

With plural nouns, use **des**:

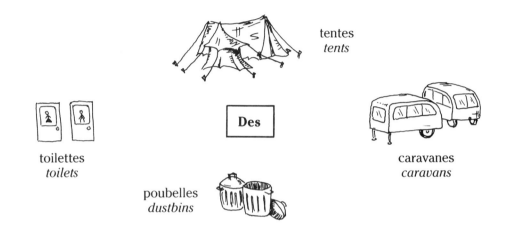

tentes *tents*

Des

toilettes *toilets*

poubelles *dustbins*

caravanes *caravans*

EXERCISE 1

Can you choose the correct word or words to go in front of these nouns?

parking
salle de télévision
tentes
bar

poubelles
snack
entrée

salle de repassage

salle de réunion
toilettes
terrain de volley

tennis

EXERCISE 2

Can you answer the following? Refer to the illustration of the campsite. Start your answer with **Il/elle est** *or* **Ils/elles sont**:

1 Où est le bureau d'accueil, s'il vous plaît?
2 Où est le parking, s'il vous plaît?
3 Où est la salle de télévision, s'il vous plaît?
4 Où se trouvent les caravanes, s'il vous plaît?
5 Où se trouve l'aire de jeux pour les enfants, s'il vous plaît?
6 Où se trouve le restaurant, s'il vous plaît?
7 Où est le bar, s'il vous plaît?
8 Où est la crêperie, s'il vous plaît?
9 Où sont les poubelles, s'il vous plaît?
10 Où sont les toilettes, s'il vous plaît?

ALLÔ! ALLÔ!

EXERCISE 3

Can you guess which rooms or other parts of the campsite you are being directed to in the following sentences? (More than one answer may be possible.)

1. Elles sont tout près des caravanes.
2. Elles sont à gauche des tentes.
3. Elle est à droite du snack.
4. Elle est à droite du terrain de pétanque.
5. Elle est en face du bureau d'accueil.
6. Elle est en face du restaurant.
7. Elles sont à gauche des caravanes.
8. Elle est à côté de la salle de repassage.
9. Il/elle est à côté de la salle de télévision.
10. Il est derrière le terrain de pétanque.

EST-CE QUE JE PEUX? *MAY I?*

This is a useful verb to know when arriving at a hotel, campsite or youth hostel. Note that it is followed by an infinitive.

Est-ce que je peux	réserver une chambre	book a room	s'il vous plaît?
	avoir un lit	have a bed	
	louer un sac de couchage	hire a sleeping bag	please?
	louer un matelas	hire a mattress	
	louer une couverture	hire a blanket	
May I	avoir un emplacement pour ma tente	have a site for my tent	
	avoir un emplacement pour ma caravane	have a site for my caravan	
	avoir deux bouteilles de camping-gaz	have two bottles of camping gas	

EXERCISE 4a

Can you complete the following? (s.v.p. *stands for* s'il vous plaît.)

1. Est-ce que je peux avoir ... s.v.p.?
2. Est-ce que je peux avoir ... s.v.p.?
3. Est-ce que je peux avoir ... s.v.p.?
4. Est-ce que je peux avoir ... s.v.p.?
5. Est-ce que je peux avoir ... s.v.p.?
6. Est-ce que je peux louer ... s.v.p.?
7. Est-ce que je peux louer ... s.v.p.?
8. Est-ce que je peux louer ... s.v.p.?
9. Est-ce que je peux réserver ... s.v.p.?
10. Est-ce que je peux réserver ... s.v.p.?

ARRIVING AT A CAMPSITE 9

OÙ EST-CE QUE JE PEUX? *WHERE CAN I?*/OÙ PEUT-ON? *WHERE CAN ONE?*

Où est-ce que je peux *Where can I* Où peut-on *Where can one*	trouver le propriétaire trouver le gardien/la gardienne trouver un garage garer la voiture monter la tente mettre les valises mettre mes/ses affaires prendre une douche acheter des provisions trouver l'auberge de jeunesse	*find the manager find the warden find a garage park the car put up the tent put the cases put my/one's things have a shower buy some food find the youth hostel*	s'il vous plaît? *please?*

EXERCISE 4b

You have just arrived at a campsite. How would you ask the questions represented by the following pictures? Try to think of as many different types of questions as you can. Your partner can try to answer them.

 ALLÔ! ALLÔ!

EXERCISE 5

«(Où) est-ce que je peux . . .?»
One of the group mimes a question which s/he might want to ask on arrival at a hotel, campsite or youth hostel, e.g.

«Est-ce que je peux avoir un sac de couchage?» *or*
«Où peut-on acheter du beurre?»

The one who guesses what the question is takes the turn instead, if s/he can give the correct French for the question.
  Or, the game may be played with two teams guessing, with a few of your best actors in front to do the miming.

  The following vocabulary may prove useful:
acheter du pain/lait/beurre/fruit/vin/de la viande/de la confiture
  to buy bread/milk/butter/fruit/wine/meat/jam
trouver le dortoir/un camping/un parking
  to find the dormitory/a campsite/a car park
louer une tente/une caravane/une chambre
  to hire a tent/a caravan/a room
réserver une chambre/un emplacement
  to book a room/a site
avoir une clef/du savon/une serviette/un oreiller de plus
  to have a key/some soap/a towel/an extra pillow

EXERCISE 6

Guess the question
Can you guess what the questions were, to which the following sentences are the answers?

EST-CE QUE JE PEUX . . .?
1 Ah oui, madame. Nous en avons une à deux lits, avec douche.
2 Non, monsieur. Je regrette, tout est complet.
3 Ah oui, monsieur. Vous pouvez la garer derrière l'hôtel.
4 Je regrette, madame, il n'y a pas de place pour les caravanes ici.
5 Oui, madame. Pour combien de nuits, et pour combien de personnes?
6 Vous en voulez combien, monsieur?
7 Oui, il y a un placement tout au fond, là-bas.

OÙ EST-CE QUE JE PEUX . . .?
8 Vous trouverez un kiosque près du parking.
9 Laissez là les valises, monsieur. On les montera pour vous.
10 Il y a une salle de bain au bout du couloir, madame.

EXERCISE 7

Can you describe these rooms?
For each room, say which floor it's on and make two more comments about beds and washing facilities.
Useful words: à un lit
       à deux lits
       avec grand lit
       il n'y a pas de . . .
       avec/sans douche
       avec/sans salle de bains
       avec lit supplémentaire

ARRIVING AT A CAMPSITE 11

C'EST COMBIEN? HOW MUCH IS IT?

C'est combien	une chambre à deux lits	a room with two beds	s'il vous
	une tente pour une nuit	a tent for one night	plaît?
How much is	un emplacement pour une caravane	a site for a caravan	please?

EXERCISE 8 *Can you ask the price of the following?*

EXERCISE 9 «C'est combien?»
Make 20 small cards, each with a picture of something you may want to buy. Turn them up one by one and test yourself. You can combine your pile with your partner's pile, and see who wins the most. You win the card if you can ask the question that goes with the picture, e.g. C'est combien, le savon?

If you want to add some luck to the game, put in a few rogue cards to say, for example, 'Give the last two/four/six cards you won to your partner', or 'Answer the next three correctly to win one', 'Miss a turn' or 'Your partner must give you three cards', etc.

ALLÔ! ALLÔ!

EXERCISE 10

With a partner, see how many questions you can make up and answer using these questions:

Est-ce que je peux . . . ?
Où est-ce que je peux . . . ?
C'est combien . . . ?

Use the hotel price list(s), the 'Camping Farret-Farinette' advertisement with its accompanying description, and the entry for the Camping l'Air Marin, using both the description and the coded signs.

Here is some help with the signs:

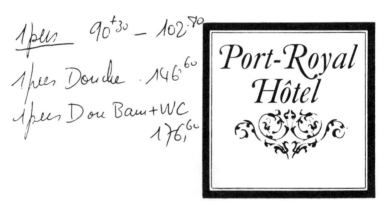

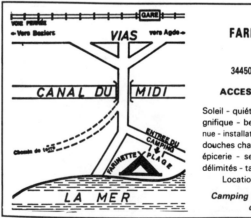

ARRIVING AT A CAMPSITE 13

Hôtels Concorde
Les Grands Hôtels de Tradition

Hôtel Concorde-St-Lazare

324 CHAMBRES ★★★★

PARIS

108, rue Saint-Lazare - 75008 PARIS
Téléphone : (1) 294.22.22 - Télex 650442

TARIF INDIVIDUEL 1985

CHAMBRE 1 PERS.	680 FF	770 FF	860 FF	950 FF
CHAMB. DOUBLE.	770 FF	860 FF	950 FF	1100 FF
LIT SUPPLEMENTAIRE				200 FF

Enfant : gratuité pour les moins de 12 ans partageant
la chambre des parents (petit déjeuner 50 FF)

PETIT DEJEUNER CONTINENTAL .... 50 FF
PETIT DEJEUNER AMERICAIN .... à la carte

Les chambres doivent être libérées à 12 h le jour du départ

T.V.A. 18,60 % incluse, service 15 % sur le hors taxe compris.
PRIX POUVANT ETRE MODIFIES SANS PREAVIS

SERVICES DE L'HOTEL

Restaurant "LE CAFE TERMINUS" - Bar "LE GOLDEN BLACK"
Service à l'étage - SALONS pour banquets, séminaires, réceptions
SALLE DE BILLARDS "D'EPOQUE"
CARTES DE CREDIT acceptées

RESERVATIONS

directement à l'Hôtel
ou à la RESERVATION CENTRALE A PARIS
24 h/24 - 7 jours/7 - Tél. : **(1) 758.12.25** - Télex 650990 F
ou de province : PCV automatique gratuit : **16 05 05 00 11**
A L'ETRANGER POUR VOS RESERVATIONS :
Bureau Local Supranational
ou votre Agent de Voyages

EXERCISE

Revision
Can you remember what to say in the following situations?

1 You can't find a hotel. **2** You can't find a campsite. **3** You're looking for a youth hostel. **4** When you arrive at a campsite, the manager is nowhere to be seen. **5** You have bought a caravan, and need a site for it. **6** You'd like a tent for two nights. **7** You arrive at a hotel. There are two of you, and you wish to stay for one night. **8** You don't know where to park the car. **9** You'd like a shower. **10** You want to go to the dormitory but you don't know where it is.

 ALLÔ! ALLÔ!

EXERCISE *Role-playing.*

1 *You have made a new friend on the beach, who is staying at a different campsite from yours. Make up a conversation in which you complain bitterly about your campsite, its discomforts and lack of amenities. Your new friend's replies show that s/he, on the contrary, is in an ideal spot.*
2 *You have just arrived at a campsite in the South of France with four friends. Ask if there is room for you for a certain number of nights, ask how much it will cost, and ask about specific amenities on the site (e.g. showers, shopping, launderette, parking space).*

CONVERSATION 1 ● At a campsite

Où se trouve le camping s'il vous plaît?	Where's the campsite, please?
This way, sir.	*Par ici, monsieur.*
Bonjour, madame. Avez-vous de la place pour une tente, s.v.p*?	Good morning, madame. Have you room for a tent, please?
For how many nights?	Pour combien de nuits?
Pour une nuit.	For one night.
Yes, monsieur. It costs 20 francs.	*Oui, monsieur. Ça coûte vingt francs.*
Ah, bon. Où est-ce qu'on règle la note?	That' fine. Where do we settle the bill?
Here, sir, at the office.	*Ici, monsieur, à la réception.*
Où est-ce que je peux monter la tente?	Where can I put up the tent?
Here, sir.	Par ici, monsieur.
Où est-ce que je peux me laver?	*Where can I wash?*
Here, sir.	Par ici, monsieur.
Où sont les toilettes?	*Where are the toilets?*
Over there, sir.	Par là, monsieur.
C'est combien, par nuit et par personne?	*How much is it for each night per person?*
50 francs, monsieur.	Cinquante francs, monsieur.
Ah, c'est trop cher. Allons à l'auberge de jeunesse. Où est mon sac de couchage?	*Oh, it's too dear. Let's go to the youth hostel. Where's my sleeping bag?*

*s.v.p = s'il vous plaît

ARRIVING AT A CAMPSITE 15

● Est-ce que je peux avoir un emplacement pour ma tente?

CONVERSATION 2 ● At an hotel

Bonsoir, madame. Est-ce que je peux vous aider?

Good evening, madame. Can I help you?

Have you any rooms, please?

Avez-vous des chambres, s.v.p?

Vous avez réservé, madame?

Have you booked, madame?

No, I haven't booked.

Non, je n'ai pas réservé.

C'est pour combien de nuits?

How many nights is it for?

Two nights. I'm leaving on Thursday.

Pour deux nuits. On part jeudi.

Vous êtes seule?

Are you alone?

No. There are two adults and two children.

Non. Nous sommes deux adultes et deux enfants.

Deux chambres à deux lits alors. Ah oui, nous en avons deux, au deuxième étage, avec douche.

Two rooms with two beds then. Ah yes, we have two, on the second floor, with shower.

How much is it?

C'est combien?

Deux cents francs, par nuit et par personne, taxe et service compris; tarif réduit pour les enfants.

200 francs per person per night, inclusive of tax and service; reduced rate for children.

16 ALLÔ! ALLÔ!

Is breakfast included?

Ah non, madame. Les repas ne sont pas compris.

It's very dear, but we'll take them.

Très bien, madame. Vous avez une pièce d'identité, s'il vous plaît?

Yes. Here are our passports. What time do you have dinner?

A huit heures à peu près, madame.

When do we settle the bill?

Quand vous voulez, madame.

Then I'd like to settle the bill now.

Très bien, madame.

Petit déjeuner compris?

Ah no, madame. Meals are not included.

C'est très cher, mais on les prend.

Very good, madame. Have you any identification, please?

Oui. Voici nos passeports. On dîne à quelle heure?

Around eight, madame.

On règle la note quand?

When you like, madame.

Je voudrais régler la note tout de suite alors.

Very good, madame.

2. Asking the way

A very useful sentence you need to know in order to ask the way is:

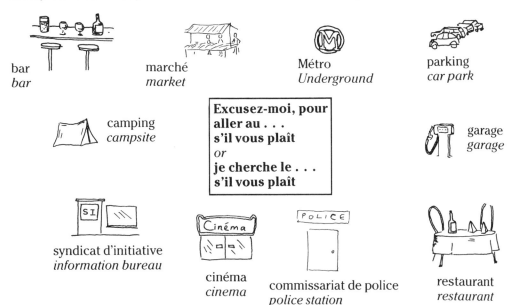

bar — *bar*
marché — *market*
Métro — *Underground*
parking — *car park*
camping — *campsite*
garage — *garage*
syndicat d'initiative — *information bureau*
cinéma — *cinema*
commissariat de police — *police station*
restaurant — *restaurant*

Excusez-moi, pour aller au . . . s'il vous plaît
or
je cherche le . . . s'il vous plaît

When the noun is feminine, you must say:

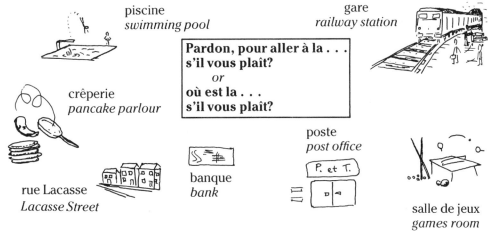

piscine — *swimming pool*
gare — *railway station*
crêperie — *pancake parlour*
rue Lacasse — *Lacasse Street*
banque — *bank*
poste — *post office*
salle de jeux — *games room*

Pardon, pour aller à la . . . s'il vous plaît?
or
où est la . . . s'il vous plaît?

When the noun begins with a vowel or h, you must say:

Excusez-moi, pour aller à  **l'hôpital** **l'église** **s'il vous plaît?**

 ALLÔ! ALLÔ!

EXERCISE 1 Can you ask the way to the following places?

EXERCISES 2 and 3 Two games. You can make up two games to practise asking the way, on the lines of Exercises 5 and 9 in lesson 1.

EXERCISE 4 Where would you ask the way to in the following situations?
  1 Your motor-bike has run out of petrol.
  2 You've had an accident and hurt your arm.
  3 You want to buy some stamps and post a card back home.
  4 You want to go for a swim.
  5 You want to change some English money.
  6 You have to catch a train.
  7 You want to see a film.
  8 You have lost your money.
  9 You're thirsty.
  10 Your car has broken down.

Where is it?

C'est It's	ici près d'ici tout près d'ici loin d'ici à droite à gauche en face	here near here very near here a long way from here on the right on the left opposite, facing you.

Here is an imaginary street:

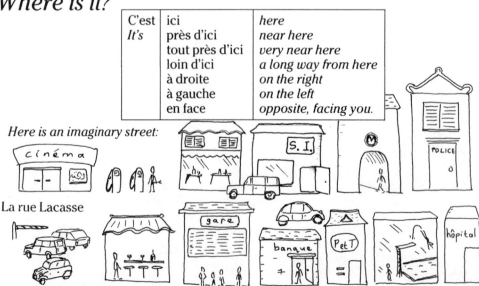

La rue Lacasse

ASKING THE WAY

Can you help the following people with their enquiries? You must tell them whether the place they are looking for is near or not, and whether it is on the right or the left, e.g.
Vous êtes près du cinema. La rue Lacasse est en face.
Enquirer: «Pour aller à la banque, s'il vous plaît?»
Answer: «C'est près d'ici, à droite.»

1 Vous êtes près du garage. La rue Lacasse est en face.
   Enquirer: «Pour aller au commissariat de police, s'il vous plaît?»
2 Vous êtes près du restaurant. La rue Lacasse est en face.
   Enquirer: «Pour aller au syndicat d'initiative, s'il vous plaît?»
3 Vous êtes près du cinéma. La rue Lacasse est en face.
   Enquirer: «Pour aller au bar, s'il vous plaît?»
4 Vous êtes près du parking. La rue Lacasse est en face.
   Enquirer: «L'hôpital est près d'ici s'il vous plaît?»
5 Vous êtes près de la gare. La rue Lacasse est en face.
   Enquirer: «La Poste est près d'ici, s'il vous plaît?»
6 Vous êtes près du commissariat de police. La rue Lacasse est derrière vous.
   Enquirer: «Pour aller à la piscine, s'il vous plaît?»
7 Vous êtes près du syndicat d'initiative. La rue Lacasse est derrière vous.
   Enquirer: «Pour aller au parking, s'il vous plaît?»
8 Vous êtes près de l'hôpital. La rue Lacasse est derrière vous.
   Enquirer: C'est loin d'ici, le garage, s'il vous plaît?»
9 Vous êtes près de la piscine. La rue Lacasse est derrière vous.
   Enquirer: «C'est près d'ici, la Poste, s'il vous plaît?»
10 Vous êtes près du Métro. La rue Lacasse est derrière vous.
   Enquirer: «Le cinéma est loin d'ici, s'il vous plaît?»

How do I reach it?

In order to help your enquirer further, you need to know the following instructions:

tournez à gauche	turn left
tournez à droite	turn right
sur votre gauche	on your left
sur votre droite	on your right
prenez à gauche	veer left
prenez à droite	veer right
allez tout droit	go straight on
droit devant vous	straight in front of you
prenez la première/ deuxième/troisième rue	take the first/second/third street
à gauche	on the left
à droite	on the right
montez la rue . . .	go up . . . Street
descendez la rue . . .	go down . . . Street
allez jusqu'au bout	go right to the end

ALLÔ! ALLÔ!

EXERCISE 6

Can you complete the following sentences?

1 Pour aller à l'hôtel Splendide,

2 Pour aller au jardin zoologique,

3 Pour aller à la crêperie,

4 Pour aller au garage,

5 Pour aller à l'hôpital,

6 Pour aller à la Poste,

7 Pour aller au bar,

8 Pour aller au bureau de port,

9 Pour aller au musée,

10 Pour aller à la gare routière,

EXERCISE 7

Where am I going? Look at the plan of the seaside town opposite. Can you tell where these people are going?

1 Je suis au carrefour. Je descends l'avenue Alphonse Daudet vers la mer. Je prends la deuxième rue à gauche. C'est tout près, sur la droite.
2 Je suis au phare. Je prends à gauche. Je vais jusqu'au bout. C'est en face.
3 Je suis à la gare routière. Je descends le boulevard de la Paix. Je prends la première rue à gauche. C'est tout près.
4 Je suis dans l'avenue Alphonse Daudet. Je monte l'avenue Molière. Je prends la deuxième rue à droite.
5 Je suis au cinéma. Je tourne à gauche au carrefour, et c'est tout de suite à droite.

ASKING THE WAY

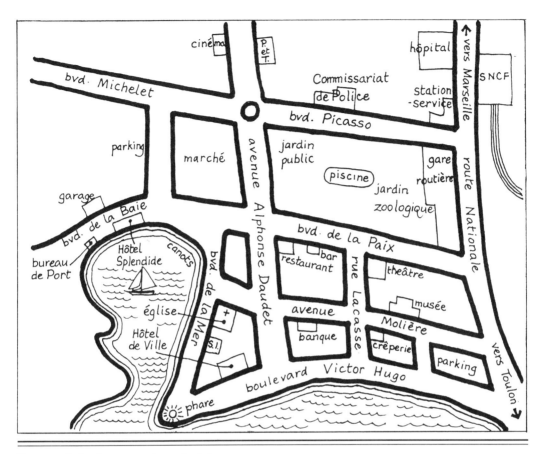

EXERCISE 8

Can you help these people to find their way in the town illustrated above? You could first tell them whether the place is nearby or not. Then use the table on page 19 to give them instructions, e.g.

Vous êtes au cinéma.
Enquirer: «Pour aller au marché s'il vous plaît?»
Answer: C'est tout près. Allez jusqu'au carrefour, tournez à droite, et le marché est sur votre gauche.»

1 Vous êtes au bureau de port.
   Enquirer: «Pour aller à la banque, s'il vous plaît?»
   Answer: «C'est ... Descendez ... jusqu'à l'avenue Alphonse Daudet, tournez à ... et prenez la ... rue à ... La banque est sur votre ...»
2 Vous êtes au bar.
   Enquirer: «Je cherche l'hôtel Splendide, s'il vous plaît?»
   Answer: C'est ... Allez jusqu'à l'avenue ... Traversez la rue. Descendez ... L'hôtel Splendide est ...»
3 Vous êtes à l'église.
   Enquirer: «Où est le phare, s'il vous plaît?»
4 Vous êtes à la gare routière.
   Enquirer: «Où se trouve la piscine, s'il vous plaît?»
5 Vous êtes au théâtre.
   Enquirer: «Pour louer des canots, s'il vous plaît?»

 ALLÔ! ALLÔ!

    6 Vous êtes à l'hôtel de ville.
       Enquirer: «Je cherche un parking, s'il vous plaît?»
    7 Vous êtes à la station-service.
       Enquirer: «Pour aller au commissariat de police, s'il vous plaît?»
    8 Vous êtes au carrefour.
       Enquirer: «Je cherche une crêperie, s'il vous plaît?»
    9 Vous êtes à la gare (S.N.C.F.)
       Enquirer: «Pour aller à la banque, s'il vous plaît?»
   10 Vous êtes au restaurant.
       Enquirer: «Où est l'hôpital, s'il vous plaît?»

EXERCISE 9

You can give yourself further practice by making a set of small cards, each containing a name mentioned on the map (l'hôpital, le phare, le jardin public, etc.) Pick up any two at random, and see if you can tell someone the way from one to the other.

You can make this into a game by having a partner. Tell your partner where the starting point is. If s/he guesses correctly from your instructions where the finishing point is, s/he wins a point; if not, you win the point. See who has the highest score out of an odd number of games.

EXERCISE 10

(on tape) Listen to the tape as it tells you where your starting point is on the town plan, and the directions you must follow. Write down what you think your point of arrival is.

EXERCISE 11

Rôle-playing
1 *You are in the main street of your own home town when a stranger comes up to you and asks you in French the way to the police station. Give him directions.*
2 *You have become separated from your friends in a small seaside town in France, and can't find the way back to your hotel. You stop someone and ask for directions, which they give you.*

EXERCISE 12

Bus routes.
Look at picture A. Imagine you are behind the counter at a tourist information bureau in Rouen. Can you read out the information about which phone numbers to ring on which days (putting the numbers into French of course!)?

JE M'INFORME SUR LE BUS

en téléphonant :

— à un seul numéro, le
35 70 20 20
de 9 h. 00 à 17 h. 00, du lundi au vendredi

— ou, en dehors de ces heures, au
35 71 63 86
Station du Théâtre des Arts, ouverte de :
5 h. 30 à 20 h. 30, du lundi au vendredi
6 h. 00 à 20 h. 30, le samedi
6 h. 30 à 20 h. 30, le dimanche.
et **35 71 81 71**
Gare Routière, ouverte tous les jours de :
6 h. 00 à 19 h. 30.

DE ROUEN
(Gare Routière)
a ISNEAUVILLE
(La Muette - Les Hauts Poiriers)

SIVOM

HORAIRE D'ETE
du
lundi 30 juin
au
dimanche 31 août
1986

LIGNES
15
150-151

Picture A

ASKING THE WAY

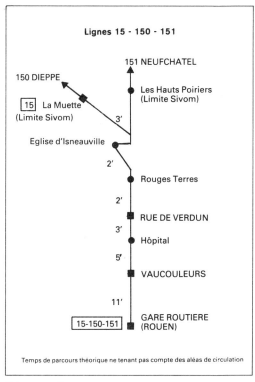

Diagram B   Card C

Look at diagram B. Can you say aloud the following sentences, completing them by referring to the diagram?

La ligne 15
La ligne 150   part de la gare routière et va jusqu'à ...
La ligne 151

Passages à Rouen, provenance   Neufchâtel,
                               Dieppe,   c'est la ligne ...
                               La Muette

                Rouen   l'Hôpital,
Pour aller de   Vaucouleurs jusqu'à   Neufchâtel   c'est la ligne ...
                La Muette   Rue de Verdun

Look at card C. Can you read out the following sentences, giving any one correct answer for each sentence?

On peut acheter le tarif plein au/à la ...
               le tarif réduit au/à la ...
               les abonnements 5 jours au/à la ...
               les coupons mensuels au/à la ...

Imagine you are behind the counter at the information bureau again. Your partner is a customer. She asks you questions about cards B and C as above; can you give the correct information?

CONVERSATION 1 • Asking the way

Pardon, monsieur. Pouvez-vous m'aider, s.v.p.?
Excuse me. Can you help me, please?

Certainly. What's the matter?
Certainement, mademoiselle. Qu'est-ce qu'il y a?

Où se trouve la Mairie, s.v.p.?
Where's the town hall, please?

Take the first street on the right.
Prenez la première rue à droite.

Pour aller à la gare, s.v.p.?
How do I get to the station, please?

Take the second street on the left.
Prenez la deuxième rue à gauche.

Pour aller au Métro, s.v.p.? C'est près d'ici?
How do I get to the Métro, please? Is it near?

Oh, yes. Go straight on.
Mais oui. Allez tout droit.

Le syndicat d'initiative est à quelle distance, s.v.p.?
How far away is the information bureau, please?

200 metres away. You have to turn left at the end of the street.
A 200 mètres. Il faut tourner à gauche au bout de la rue.

Y a-t-il un arrêt d'autobus près d'ici? C'est loin?
Is there a bus stop near here? Is it far?

It's about 2 kilometres away.
C'est à deux kilometres, à peu près.

Et où est la banque la plus proche?
And where's the nearest bank?

It's 100 metres away.
Il y en a une à cent mètres.

Merci beaucoup, monsieur.
Thank you very much.

Not at all. Would you like me to go with you?
De rien, mademoiselle. Voulez-vous que je vous accompagne?

Non merci, monsieur. Ce n'est pas la peine. Au revoir, m...
No thank you. It's not worth the trouble. Goodbye.

Goodbye.
Au revoir, m...

ASKING THE WAY 25

CONVERSATION 2 — I can't understand!

Pardon, madame. Pour aller rue Lacasse, s.v.p.?

Excuse me, madame, how do I get to rue Lacasse, please?

Il vaut mieux y aller en autobus. Il y a un arrêt d'autobus tout près.

You'd better go by bus. There's a bus stop very near.

Voulez-vous répéter, madame? Je ne comprends pas.

Will you say that again, madame? I don't understand.

Prenez l'autobus.

Take the bus.

Ah bon. Et pour trouver l'autobus?

Oh I see. And how do I find the bus?

Pour ça, il faut tourner à droite, tourner à gauche et aller tout droit.

For that, you have to turn right, turn left and go straight on.

Voulez-vous parler plus lentement, madame? Je n'ai pas compris.

Will you speak more slowly, madame? I didn't understand.

Vous n'avez pas compris? Et bien – prenez le Métro.

You didn't understand? Well then – take the Métro.

Ah bon. Et pour aller au Métro?

Oh I see. And how do I get to the Métro?

Pour aller au Métro, traversez la rue, tout simplement.

To get to the Métro, just cross the road.

Comment, madame? Je n'ai pas compris.

Pardon? I didn't understand.

Ça alors! Il vaut mieux y aller en taxi.

Good heavens! You'd better go by taxi.

Comment madame?

Pardon?

PRENEZ UN TAXI!

GET A TAXI!

Ah bon. Finalement, j'ai compris – il faut prendre un taxi . . . et pour prendre un taxi?

Oh I see. I've understood at last – I have to get a taxi . . . and how do I get a taxi?

(SCREAM. . .)

3 Shopping

A game – 'Happy Tomatoes'

This is a variation of the old 'Happy Families' game, to get you used to the vocabulary you will need for shopping in France. You need to make 4 cards for each shop. Each card illustrates a different article which may be bought at that shop, e.g.

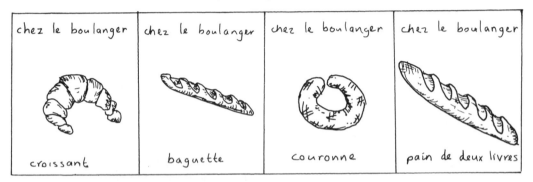

The cards are shuffled and divided among three or four players. The dealer begins. The aim is to complete as many sets of 4 cards as you can. The winner is the one with the most sets when all the 'families' are complete.

If, for example, the dealer has a croissant *from the* boulanger *family, he will say to any of the others:* 'Boulanger – baguette?' *or* 'Boulanger – couronne?' *or* 'Boulanger – pain de deux livres?' *If that person has the card asked for, he or she must give it up. The dealer continues to have turns until he makes a wrong guess as to the whereabouts of any card. The turn is then taken by the one whom the dealer asked unsuccessfully for a card.*

Here are some suggestions for the "families" you can make; invent more of your own if you like.

chez le boucher:	steak	côte d'agneau	canard	poulet
at the butcher's	*steak*	*lamb chop*	*duck*	*chicken*
chez le charcutier	bacon	côte de porc	charcuterie	pâté
at the pork butcher's	*bacon*	*pork chop*	*cold cooked meat*	*pate, meat paste*
chez le confisier	bonbons	chocolat	nougat	chewing-gum
at the sweet shop	*sweets*	*chocolate*	*nougat*	*chewing-gum*
chez l'épicier	vin	eau minérale	boîte de pêches	paquet de biscuits
at the grocer's	*wine*	*mineral water*	*tin of peaches*	*packet of biscuits*
chez le marchand de fruits	bananes	oranges	pommes	fraises
at the fruiterer's	*bananas*	*oranges*	*apples*	*strawberries*
chez le marchand de légumes	pommes de terre	pois	haricots	chou-fleur
at the greengrocer's	*potatoes*	*peas*	*beans*	*cauliflower*
chez le papetier	papier à lettres	enveloppe	carte postale	stylo
at the stationer's	*writing paper*	*envelope*	*post card*	*biro*

SHOPPING 27

chez le pâtissier	biscuits	gâteaux	glace	brioche
at the cake shop	*biscuits*	*cakes*	*ice-cream*	*bun*
chez le pharmacien	aspirine	sparadrap	pellicule	médicaments
at the chemist's	*aspirin*	*plaster*	*film*	*medicine*
chez le poissonnier	sardines	hareng	saumon	truite
at the fish shop	*sardines*	*herring*	*salmon*	*trout*
au kiosque de journaux	journal	magazine	hebdomadaire	bandes dessinées
at the newspaper kiosk	*newspaper*	*magazine*	*weekly*	*strip cartoons*
au supermarché	chips	parfum	disque	jean
at the supermarket	*crisps*	*perfume*	*record*	*jeans*
au café-tabac	cigarettes	allumettes	briquet	timbres
at the cafe-cum-tobacconist's	*cigarettes*	*matches*	*lighter*	*stamps*
à la Poste	mandat postal	timbres	carte postale	colis
at the Post Office	*postal order*	*stamps*	*post card*	*parcel*

The game of pairs

This is another well-known memory game. Cut out 40 squares about 3 cm square from paper or card, and on each pair of cards draw the identical item of food. Write the names on the cards in French. You may have two apples, two loaves, two ice-creams, etc. The vocabulary on the previous page will be useful.

Shuffle the cards and lay them face down on the table. The first player picks up any two, and reads out the names on the cards. If they are identical, s/he keeps them, and has another turn. If s/he doesn't find a pair, it is the partner's turn. The idea is that you memorise the positions of the different articles, so that when you pick up a new card, you can remember where the other half of the pair is.

If you want to make the game more difficult, don't name the cards. In order to win the pair, you and your partner must not only find them, but give the correct French name also.

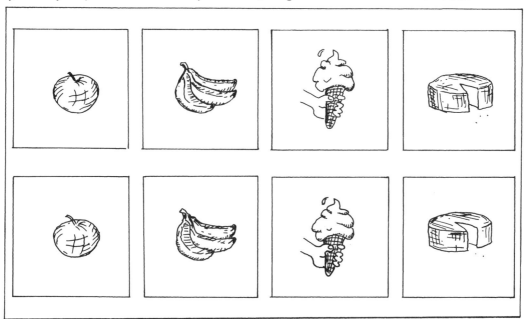

 ALLÔ! ALLÔ!

How much is it?

C'est combien	le pain?	(the) bread?
Ça coûte combien	le fromage?	(the) cheese?
How much is (are)	l'eau minérale?	(the) mineral water?
	la limonade?	(the) lemonade?
	les saucisses?	(the) sausages?
	les pommes de terre?	(the) potatoes?

EXERCISE *Can you ask the price of the following articles?*

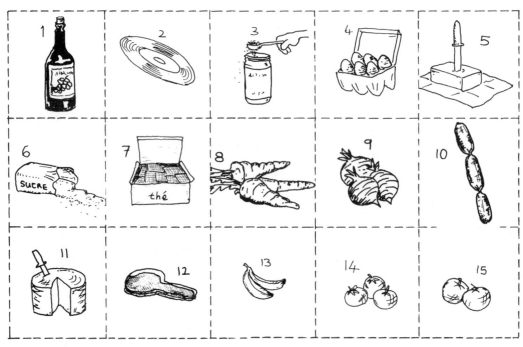

Saying how much it is

Un	1		le kilo *a kilo*	
deux	2		la bouteille *a bottle*	
trois	3		la pièce *each*	
quatre	4	francs	la boîte *a tin*	
cinq	5		le paquet *a packet*	
six	6		la livre *a lb*	
sept	7		la douzaine *a dozen*	
dix	10	centimes		
vingt	20			
trente	30			
quarante	40			
cinquante	50			
cent	100			

SHOPPING (29)

EXERCISE 2

You need a partner for this exercise. One of you asks the price of the article, and the other replies, according to the information given in the illustrations.
E.g. C'est combien, le disque?
Ans. Soixante francs.

1	2	3	4	5
60 f.	30 f.	1k 2f.50	1k 9f	10f.30

6	7	8	9	10
1k 8f.30	1k 4f.20	1k 5f.	6f.	10f.

11	12	13	14	15
5f.	13f.	1k 12f.	20f.	18f.50

EXERCISE 3

A game for two. For this you need eleven cards marked with prices between 1 and 11 francs, and eleven cards, each illustrating a different article of food. These can be cut from magazines.
  The 'shopkeeper' has the pile showing articles of food, and the 'customer' has the prices. Both piles are upside down. The shopkeeper offers for sale one of the articles of food, and the customer must ask how much it is in correct French. The shopkeeper guesses any price between 1 and 11 francs.
  The customer picks up his top card, and if the price on it is what the shopkeeper stated to within 3 francs, the shopkeeper wins the article of food; otherwise, the customer wins it. The customer shuffles his cards of prices, and the shopkeeper holds up the next article for sale.
  Put in some 'wild cards' if you like, with instructions such as 'give 1/2/3 cards to your partner'.
  The conversation would go something like this:
Shopkeeper: Vous voulez des carottes, monsieur/mademoiselle?
Customer: C'est combien, les carottes?
Shopkeeper (guessing): 3 francs
Customer (seeing that the top card shows 7 francs): Vous avez perdu. *(S/he keeps the card.)*
or

Customer (seeing that the top card shows 6 francs or less): Vous avez gagné. *(S/he gives the card to the shopkeeper.)*
The winner is the one who has the larger pile of food at the end of the game.

Where do you buy it?

 le pharmacien
the chemist's

le papetier
the stationer's

 le confisier
the sweet shop

le charcutier
the pork butcher's

Chez

 le marchand de légumes
the greengrocer's (for vegetables)

le marchand de fruits
the greengrocer's (for fruit)

le boulanger
the baker's

l'épicier
the grocer's

le pâtissier
the confectioner's

le poissonnier
the fish shop
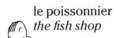

le boucher
the butcher

SHOPPING

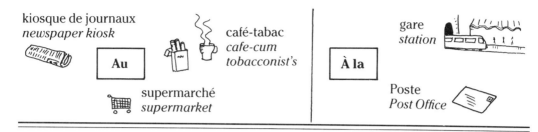

EXERCISE 4

At the wrong shop. In each of the following situations, you are in the wrong shop. When you ask if the article is sold there, the assistant says. «Ah, non, il faut aller . . .» and you must insert the name of the correct shop. E.g.:
Chez le boulanger.
Vous vendez des tomates?
Answer: Ah non, il faut aller chez le marchand de légumes.

1 Chez le boucher. Vous vendez des bananes?
2 Chez le pharmacien. Vous vendez des journaux?
3 Chez le confisier. Vous vendez des timbres?
4 Chez le pâtissier. Vous vendez du tabac?
5 Chez le marchand de légumes. Vous vendez du beurre?
6 A la Poste. Vous vendez du papier à lettres?
7 Chez le poissonnier. Vous vendez des saucisses?
8 Chez l'épicier. Vous vendez du saumon?
9 Chez le papetier. Vous vendez des croissants?
10 Au café-tabac. Vous vendez des choux?

Alternative names of shops

Chez le boulanger *really means 'at the house of the baker'. Another way of saying 'at the baker's' is* **à la boulangerie.**
The following list gives you the alternative names of some shops:

chez le boulanger	à la boulangerie	chez le papetier	à la papeterie
chez le boucher	à la boucherie	chez le pâtissier	à la pâtisserie
chez le charcutier	à la charcuterie	chez le pharmacien	à la pharmacie
chez le confisier	à la confiserie	chez le poissonnier	à la poissonnerie
chez l'épicier	à l'épicerie		

EXERCISE 5

Complete the blanks in the following sentences:

1 Je vais . . . car je veux acheter des cartes postales.
2 Je vais . . . car je dois acheter du sparadrap.
3 Je vais . . . car je n'ai pas de bananes.
4 Je vais . . . car j'ai besoin de timbres.
5 Je vais . . . car je dois trouver un disque pour l'anniversaire de mon cousin.
6 Je vais . . . car il me faut du saumon.
7 Je vais . . . car je n'ai plus de pommes.
8 Je vais . . . car maman veut des bonbons.
9 Je vais . . . car il me faut du vin pour ce soir.
10 Je vais . . . pour acheter de l'aspirine, car j'ai mal à la tête.

 ALLÔ! ALLÔ!

In the shop

deux cents grammes de bonbons
200 grammes of sweets

un kilo de bacon
a kilo of bacon

une boîte de pêches
a tin of peaches

> **Je voudrais**
> *I'd like*
> **Donnez-moi**
> *Give me*
> **Je prends**
> *I'll have*

une douzaine d'œufs
a dozen eggs

une bouteille de vin
a bottle of wine

un paquet de biscuits
a packet of biscuits

EXERCISE 6

For this exercise you and your friend take the parts of a person shopping and a helpful stranger. This is the sort of conversation you can have:

Shopper
Pardon, m..., où est-ce que je peux acheter du pain, s.v.p.?

Où se trouve la boulangerie, s.v.p.?

In the shop
Donnez-moi deux baguettes, s.v.p.

Stranger
Il faut aller à la boulangerie (*or* chez le boulanger).

Prenez la rue à gauche/droite et c'est entre la Poste et le cinéma (*vary these answers*).

Assistant
Voilà, m... Ça fait 10 francs.

Use these illustrations to guide you:

 1   2   3   4   5

 6    7   8   9   10

SHOPPING 33

EXERCISE 7

Listen to Conversation 1 on the tape. Then with a partner make up your own conversations based on the first part of the tape. Refer to the plan of Le Printemps *and the* emplacement des rayons. *Decide which department, shop and floor you need for your purchases before you start. One of you can be the customer and the other the guide.*

The articles you want to buy are as follows: some tights – writing paper – soap – a necklace – a dog's collar – some chocolates – a tie. This will require 7 conversations. You can use the following pattern to help you:

«Où est le rayon des *(which department?)* s'il vous plaît?»
    «C'est dans le *(which shop?)*»
«Ah bon. Et c'est à quel étage, s'il vous plaît?»
    «C'est au *(which floor?)*»
«Merci beaucoup.»

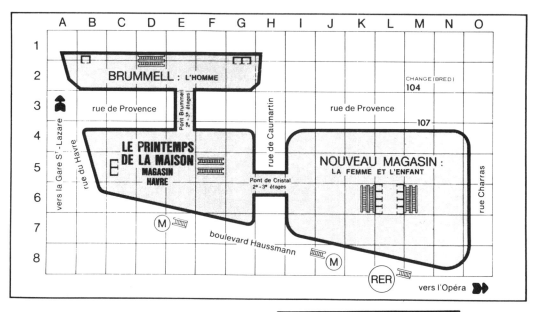

Printemps
Brummell
plan des rayons

Ce plan est régulièrement remis à jour. A votre prochaine visite, n'oubliez pas d'en prendre un nouveau.

EMPLACEMENT DES RAYONS			
RAYONS	MAGASIN	ETAGE	PLAN
Accessoires de mode	nouveau	RC	
accueil - information	nouveau	RC	J 4
adoption animaux	havre	6e	B 6
agence de voyages	nouveau	6e	M 5
animaux : accessoires	nouveau	ss-sol	L 6
articles de bureau	havre	ss-sol	
articles de ménage	nouveau	ss-sol	J 7
articles de sport, tennis, omnisport...	nouveau	ss-sol	M 5
Baby	nouveau	5e	M 6
bagages	havre	3e	D 6
bas pour dames	nouveau	RC	N 6
bébés : vêtements-puériculture	nouveau	5e	N 4
bijouterie fantaisie	nouveau	RC	N 8
bijouterie joaillerie	havre	RC	C 4
bonneterie enfants	nouveau	5e	N 7
boutique blanche (listes de mariage)	havre	2e	C 5
boutique douce (épicerie fine, confiserie)	nouveau	6e	L 7
boutons	nouveau	6e	J 4
brosserie fine	havre	RC	C 5
brummell : vêtements et accessoires pour hommes	nouveau brummell	RC	N 4

ALLÔ! ALLÔ!

EXERCISE 8

Revision
1 *Ask for some ham for six people.* 2 *Ask if they sell bread.* 3 *Ask if they also sell fruit juice.* 4 *Ask if they have any croissants.* 5 *Ask for a kilo of bananas.* 6 *Ask how much you owe.* 7 *Ask if you can buy butter at this shop.* 8 *Ask if they have any tins of peaches.* 9 *Ask if the shop's closed today.* 10 *Ask if the shop's open today.* 11 *Ask how much the tomatoes cost.* 12 *Ask how much the jeans in the window* (la vitrine) *cost.* 13 *Ask how much the croissants cost.* 14 *Tell someone to go to the post office.* 15 *Tell someone to go to the newspaper kiosk.* 16 *Ask where you can buy bread.* 17 *Ask where you can buy a tie.* 18 *Ask where you can buy some stamps.* 19 *Ask how to get to the supermarket.* 20 *Ask how to get to the confectioner's.*

EXERCISE 9

Rôle-playing.
1 *You've just arrived at a campsite, and have no food. Go into the campsite's general store, and buy what you need for yourself and your friends for an evening meal and breakfast the following morning.*
2 *Buy in a grocer's shop the items you need for a picnic for four people.*

CONVERSATION 1 ● At the department store

Excusez-moi, où est l'agence de voyages, s.v.p.?	*Excuse me, where's the travel agency, please?*
It's in the new shop.	Elle dans le nouveau magasin.
Ah bon. Et c'est à quel étage?	*I see. And what floor is it on?*
It's on the 6th floor.	C'est au sixième étage.
Il y a un ascenseur?	*Is there a lift?*
No, just an escalator. It's near the cash desk over there.	Non, un escalier roulant seulement. C'est près de la caisse là-bas.
Il n'y a pas d'escalier?	*Isn't there a staircase?*
Oh yes. There's a staircase near the exit.	Ah si. Il y a un escalier près de la sortie.
Merci beaucoup, madame.	*Thank you very much, madame.*
Not at all.	De rien, monsieur/mademoiselle.

SHOPPING

CONVERSATION 2 • Buying a present

Je peux vous aider, m . . .?

Have you a pullover, size 40, please?

De quelle couleur?

I don't mind.

Vous le voulez en coton, en laine ou en nylon?

Wool, please.

En voici un à 200 francs.

Oh no, it's too dear. Haven't you any cheaper?

Et bien, voici un très joli Tee-shirt en coton à 30 francs.

Oh yes. It's nice, I'll have it.

C'est pour offrir?

Yes. It's for my sister. Can you gift-wrap it please?

Certainement, m . . . Voilà.

Thank you very much. I shall certainly come back. Are you open every day?

On ferme la dimanche seulement. On ouvre à neuf heures tous les jours et on ferme à 17 heures.

Thank you, m . . . Goodbye.

Au revoir, m . . .

Can I help you, m . . .?

Je voudrais un pull, taille 40, s.v.p.?

What colour?

Ça n'a pas d'importance.

Do you want it in cotton, wool or nylon?

En laine, s.v.p.

Here's one at 200 francs.

Ah non, c'est trop cher. Vous n'en avez pas de moins cher?

Well, here's a very nice cotton T-shirt for 30 francs.

Ah oui. Il est joli. Je le prends.

Is it for a present?

Oui. C'est pour ma soeur. Pouvez-vous me faire un paquet-cadeau, s.v.p.?

Certainly, m . . . There you are.

Merci beaucoup. Je vais certainement revenir. Vous ouvrez tous les jours?

We only close on Sundays. We open at 9 o'clock every day and close at 5 p.m.

Merci, m . . . Au revoir.

Goodbye, m . . .

CONVERSATION 3 • Shopping for food

Vous désirez, monsieur?	*Can I help you?*
A litre of milk, please.	Un litre de lait, s.v.p.
Voilà. Et avec ça?	*There you are. Anything else?*
A kilo of butter, please.	Un kilo de beurre, s.v.p.
Voilà. Et avec ça?	*There. Anything else?*
Six tomatoes, please.	Six tomates, s.v.p.
Voilà. Et avec ça?	*There. Anything else?*
Two slices of ham, please.	Deux tranches de jambon, s.v.p.
Voilà. Et avec ça?	*There. Anything else?*
A packet of biscuits, please.	Un paquet de biscuits, s.v.p.
Voilà. Et avec ça?	*There. Anything else?*
A pot of jam, please.	Un pot de confiture, s.v.p.
Voilà. Et avec ça?	*There. Anything else?*
100 grammes of sweets, please.	Cent grammes de bonbons, s.v.p.
Voilà. Et avec ca?	*There. Anything else?*
Have you any cheese, please?	Avez-vous du fromage, s.v.p.?
Oui, bien sûr. Lequel voulez-vous?	*Yes, sure. Which one do you want?*
I'll have this one, please . . . Oh no, I prefer that one.	Je prends celui-ci, s.v.p. . . . Ah non. Je préfère celui-là.
Voilà. C'est tout?	*There you are. Is that all?*
Yes, that's all, thank you. How much do I owe you?	Oui, c'est tout, merci. Je vous dois combien?
Ça fait soixante francs, s.v.p.	*That's 60 francs in all, please.*
Here's a 100-franc note.	Voilà un billet de cent francs.
Et voilà quarante francs que je vous rends.	*And there's 40 francs change.*
Excuse me, madame. It's not right.	Excusez-moi, madame, ce n'est pas juste.
Comment, ce n'est pas juste?	*What do you mean, it's not right?*
I owe you 60 francs.	Je vous dois soixante francs.
C'est ça.	*That's right.*
I gave you 100 francs.	Je vous ai donné cent francs.
C'est ça.	*That's right.*
You have to give me 40 francs change.	Il faut me rendre 40 francs.
Parfaitement!	*Exactly.*

SHOPPING (37)

You only gave me 4 francs back.	Vous m'avez rendu 4 francs seulement.
Oh, excusez-moi ... Je suis vraiment désolé(e). Voici encore 36 francs.	*Oh, forgive me. I'm very sorry. Here's another 36 francs.*
Thank you, madame.	Merci, madame.

EXERCISE 10

Choose a partner. One of you is a tourist asking for information, and the other one is a resident. When the tourist asks a question, the resident can answer by referring to the advertisements round the map on the next page.

The tourist asks where something can be bought. The reply will be one of the shops, hotels or eating places advertised. Then s/he asks the way there, and must be given directions.

Here are some useful questions to start these conversations:

1 Excusez-moi, où est-ce que je peux acheter des fleurs, s'il vous plaît? (Vous êtes à la gare.)
2 Excusez-moi, où est-ce que je peux acheter des magazines, s'il vous plaît? (Vous êtes au syndicat d'initiative.)
3 Excusez-moi, savez-vous où je peux acheter de la viande, s'il vous plaît? (Vous êtes au nouveau port.)
4 Excusez-moi, pouvez-vous me dire où je peux acheter une pierre tombale, s'il vous plaît? (Vous êtes à l'hôpital.)
4 J'ai grande envie de goûter les anguilles. Est-ce que vous pouvez me recommander un restaurant, s'il vous plaît? (Vous êtes à la mairie.)
5 J'ai besoin d'un maillot de bain. Où est-ce que je peux en acheter un, s'il vous plaît? (Vous êtes au jardin public.)
6 Je voudrais acheter des espadrilles. Où est-ce que je peux en trouver, s'il vous plaît? (Vous êtes au parking.)
7 Pardonnez-moi, pouvez-vous me dire où je peux trouver un snack qui sert des pizzas, s'il vous plaît? (Vous êtes au Clos des Plages.)
8 Excusez-moi, est-ce que vous connaissez le nom d'un hôtel situé près de la mer, s'il vous plaît?
9 Excusez-moi, je cherche un petit hôtel confortable, mais pas trop cher, s'il vous plaît. (Vous êtes à la gare.)
10 Excusez-moi, pouvez-vous me dire s'il y a un Casino ici, s'il vous plaît? (Vous êtes à la gare.)
11 Est-ce qu'il y a un self-service pas trop loin d'ici, s'il vous plaît? (Vous êtes au syndicat d'initiative.)

You can also ask where to play golf, where to post your letters, where to park your car, where to go if you have hurt your arm, where to catch the train, etc.

38 ALLÔ! ALLÔ!

Hotel ** NN
Beau Soleil

Bar-Brasserie
restaurant
Gilles de Retz
Quai Leray
Ouvert toute
l'année

La Flavinière
Ses chambres confortables - Ses repas soignés - Son jardin agréable
FLAVIEN POIRET *(Propriétaire)*
Tél.: 350   AU CLOS DES PLAGES   LA CIOTAT
R. C. Marseille 152 284   TRAMWAYS Ste-MARGUERITE

ENTREPRISE DE MAÇONNERIE
Louis GASPARINI
AVENUE N° 4
Tél.: 404   LE CLOS DES PLAGES

Société Brasserie Casino
"Les Flots Bleus"
Ouvert toute l'année   -   Grande terrasse au bord de mer
TÉLÉPHONE : 063

Chez Tintin
Grill-Restaurant
Spécialités:
Eté: la Paëlla
Hiver: les
   Anguilles
rue Foch
Ouvert toute
l'année

BOUCHERIE PARISIENNE
MAISON PAUL
Tél.: 78 - 7, RUE FÉLIX-PYAT, 7 - LA CIOTAT
VIANDES DE PREMIER CHOIX
Succursales à CEYRESTE, Rue Louis-Cruvelier - Tél.: 4

PAUL CHAUSSEUR
27, Quai du Général-De-Gaulle 27. — LA CIOTAT
ARTICLES POUR HOMMES - FEMMES ET ENFANTS
Sports - De la fantaisie - De l'élégance - De la qualité - Plage

---

Crèperie-Snack-Bar
"Le Courant d'air
Pizza-Jeux
Fast Food
Nouveau Port
Ouvert toute l'année
jusqu'a 2 heures
du matin

LES CHAUSSURES DE ROMANS
L. CAZES
32, Quai du Général DE GAULLE, 32
Prix modérés   LUXE - FANTAISIE - TRAVAIL

JACQUES COURTY
Libraire - Papetier
ENTRÉ LIBRE -:- 42, Rue des Poilus, 42

FLEURS
SPÉCIALITÉS DE FLEURS COUPÉES
FRANÇOIS TROTOBAS
Place Esquiros (prés P. T. T.)   -o-   Tél.: 347
CRÉATION & FOURNITURES DE JARDINS

L'Ecu de France
sur le Vieux Port
Self-service
Dégustation-
Fruits de mer

4) Travel by train, coach or plane

Finding your way on the Métro:

On the Métro, each **ligne** has two **directions.** To find your **direction,** follow the line through from the station where you are, through the station you want to go to, to the end of the line. The last station on the line (shown in a box) gives you your **direction.**

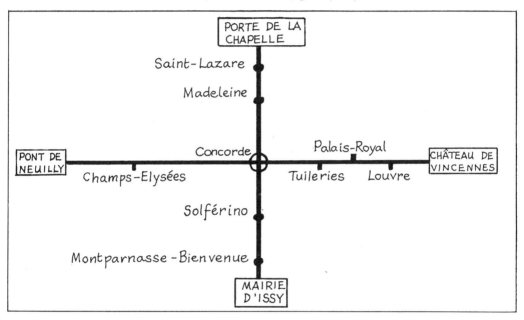

Asking the way on the Métro

EXERCISE 1

Choose a partner. One of you is the traveller, and the other the counter clerk. The traveller asks these questions:

Pour aller à ... s'il vous plaît, faut-il changer de train?
(*Answer*: Oui, à ... *or* Non, ce n'est pas nécessaire.)
Je dois prendre quelle direction?
(*Answer*: (name in a box), puis (another name in a box, if you have to change trains).)

Here are your journeys:

1. St-Lazare *to* Palais-Royal.
2. St-Lazare *to* Montparnasse-Bienvenue.
3. Solférino *to the* Champs-Elysées.
4. Solférino *to* Madeleine.
5. The Champs-Elysées *to the* Louvre.
6. *The* Louvre *to* Concorde.
7. *The* Tuileries *to* St-Lazare.
8. Palais-Royal *to* Solférino.
9. Madeleine *to the* Tuileries.
10. Concorde *to* Montparnasse-Bienvenue.

 ALLÔ! ALLÔ!

Useful vocabulary

le carnet (de tickets)	a booklet of tickets
le portillon automatique	the automatic barrier
la rame	the train
la station	the station (on the Métro)
prendre une correspondance	to get a connection
interdit de fumer	smoking is forbidden

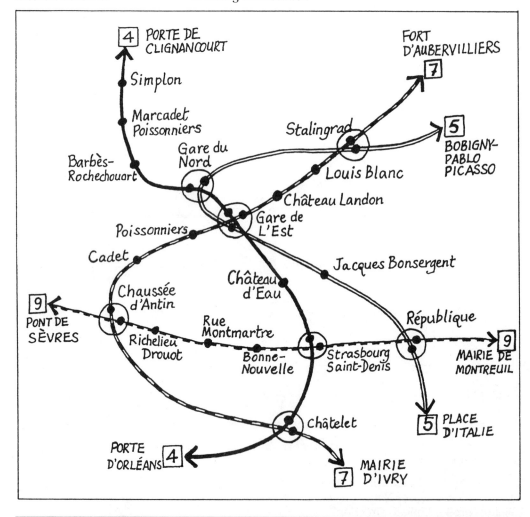

Look at the map above, and note that each line (**ligne**) has a number (**numéro**) and two directions (**directions**). The stations where you can change lines are marked with a large circle.

Take turns with your partner to be the puzzled traveller ('Excusez-moi, M..., pour aller de la gare du Nord jusqu' à Cadet, je dois prendre quelle ligne, s'il vous plaît?') and the helpful passer-by, who may say something like 'Il faut prendre la ligne numéro 4, direction Porte d'Orléans, jusqu' à la gare de l'Est. Puis il faut prendre la ligne numéro 7, direction Mairie d'Ivry.'

TRAVEL 41

One of you can prepare the answers for questions 1, 3, 5, 7, 9 and the other the answers for 2, 4, 6, 8, 10. Then you should be able to hold quite rapid conversations.

1 *From* Marcadet Poissonniers *to* la gare de l'Est.
2 *From* la gare de l'Est *to* Stalingrad.
3 *From* Richelieu Drouot *to* la gare de l'Est.
4 *From* Richelieu Drouot *to* la gare du Nord.
5 *From* Richelieu Drouot *to* République.
6 *From* République *to* Bonne Nouvelle.
7 *From* République *to* Cadet.
8 *From* Cadet *to* Simplon.
9 *From* Château Landon *to* Strasbourg Saint-Denis.
10 *From* Jacques Bonsergent *to* Stalingrad.

Buying a ticket on the Métro, railway or bus

EXERCISE 3

Listen to the first part of Conversation 1 on the tape. If you buy a ticket in this way, you will drive the counter clerk mad! He's in a hurry. Can you buy the following tickets, stating all your requirements in one sentence?

How many tickets?	Single or return	Class	Destination	Date	S'il v. plaît	Ask how much
1	⟶	2	Versailles	today	s.v.p.	?
3	⟵⟶	2	Nice	today	s.v.p.	?
2	⟶	1	Grasse	tomorrow	s.v.p.	?
1 adult + 2 children	⟶	1	Lyon	today	s.v.p.	?
2	⟵⟶	reduced price	Biarritz	1 March	s.v.p.	?
a booklet	–	–	–	–	s.v.p.	?

E.g. «Un aller simple, à tarif rèduit, pour Marseille, s'il vous plaît. C'est combien?».

How much is it?

EXERCISE 4

Your partner is behind the desk at a travel agency. You are asking for the price of the journeys listed below. Your partner will give you the prices according to the information on the advertisement. If you like, you can test yourself further by not looking at the advertisement, and trying to write down the prices s/he gives you. Remember to say «C'est combien, s'il vous plaît?» at the end of each enquiry. Ask for the following:

1 Quimper-Londres, aller-retour, adulte.
2 Morlaix-Londres, aller-retour, enfant.
3 Rennes-Caen, aller-retour journée, adulte.

4 Morlaix-Cork, aller-retour, enfant.
5 Caen-Londres, aller-retour, deux enfants.

TRAVEL 43

Making a reservation

```
SNCF                                              Réservation  classe 2

Départ    12.08 PARIS GARE DE LYON       Train      755 TGV    Voiture  05
                                      01 Places  11
Arrivée   14.18 DIJON VILLE

Date      LE 21.05.82                                          DC

          8709100575   Particularités SALLE NON FUMEURS                  Prix
          015                         1 FENETRE          ASSISE  00  01
                054324
          PARIS LYON
          21.05.82  50
                                                                    F*****8,00

          7016 0015 03827823
```

Choose a partner. One of you is behind the counter at a French travel agency, and asks the following questions:

   votre nom, s.v.p.?
   nombre de passagers?
   aller simple ou aller retour?
   classe?
   destination?
   heure du départ?
   date?
   prestations?
   particularités?

The other partner starts by saying «Je veux réserver 1 (ou 2) place(s) pour Strasbourg (etc.) s'il vous plaît»
Then s/he gives the answers, according to the notes below:

   a-s = aller simple
   a-r = aller-retour
   Mlle Junot, 1 a-s, 1ère, Strasbourg, 8.00, 1 mai, assise, couloir.
   Mme. Sàlut, 2, a-r, seconde, Marseille, 9.15, 2 juin, place pour voiture, fenêtre.
   M. Gervais, 2, a-s, 1ère, Nice, 20.45, 4 août, voitures-lits, salle fumeurs.
   M. Rolle, 1, a-r, 1ère, Evian, 21.30, 3 juillet, couchette, salle non fumeurs.

When your partner asks the questions, give answers of your own, which s/he must then jot down in English. S/he can read them back to you to see if s/he got them right!

 ALLÔ! ALLÔ!

When shall we get there?

Relations intérieures en provenances (ou à destination) des ports de la Manche

30 Dieppe/Oissel (Rouen) ▶ Avignon/Fréjus-St-Raphaël TAC et TMA

service assuré
● du 16 juin au 15 septembre : les lundis
acceptation des véhicules
Dieppe, de 17 h 30 à 19 h
Oissel, de 17 h 30 à 20 h
mise à disposition
Avignon-Fontcouverte, à partir de 7 h 30 jusqu'à 13 h (🚌 à 7 h 05)
Fréjus-St-Raphaël, à partir de 10 h 15 jusqu'à 19 h 30

horaires	n° du train	9654
Dieppe-Ville		19 52
Oissel		21 13
Avignon-Ville		6 49
Fréjus-St-Raphaël		9 40

prestations
⊢ 2ᵉ
🛏 Sp, T2

30 Fréjus-St-Raphaël/Avignon ▶ Oissel (Rouen)/Dieppe TAC et TMA

service assuré
● du 14 juin au 13 septembre : les samedis
acceptation des véhicules
Fréjus-St-Raphaël, de 15 h jusqu'à 17 h 40
Avignon-Fontcouverte, de 18 h 30 à 21 h
mise à disposition
Oissel, à partir de 9 h 30 jusqu'à 12 h
Dieppe, à partir de 10 h jusqu'à 12 h

horaires	n° du train	9634
Fréjus-St-Raphaël		18 33
Avignon-Fontcouverte		21 40
Oissel		8 18
Dieppe-Ville		9 37

prestations
⊢ 2ᵉ
🛏 Sp, T2
🍴 de Fréjus à Lyon

Signes et abréviations

TAC	train autos couchettes	⊢	couchette 1-2
SAE	service autos express	🛏	voiture-lit :
TAJ	train autos jour		(S) Single
TAM	train motos accompagnées		(Sp) Spécial
✕	voiture-restaurant		(D) Double
⊗	libre-service, gril-express		(T2) Touriste
🍱	plateau-repas		(T3) Touriste
⏏	bar, bar-corail		(T4) Touriste
🍴	restauration ambulante	🚌	autocar de liaison
			(voir ci-dessus)
(HEC)	Heure de l'Europe Centrale	👪	offre familles
			(voir p. 3)

Renseignements et horaires donnés (en heure locale) sous réserve de toute modification.

EXERCISE

Choose a partner. One of you asks the following questions:

Pour aller à Fréjus-St-Raphael, on part de Dieppe-Ville (*or* Oissel *or* Avignon-Ville) à quelle heure?
Et on arrive à Oissel/Avignon-Ville/Fréjus-St-Raphael à quelle heure?

TRAVEL (45)

The other one answers from the information given on the timetable. You can do the same for the return journey.
  Then you can ask other questions, e.g.

Quel est le numéro du train?
Est-ce qu'il y a des couchettes? En quelle classe?
Est-ce qu'il y a un grill-express?
Que veut dire TAC?
Que veut dire TAM?
Est-ce qu'il y a des voiture-lits? En quelle classe?
Est-ce qu'il y a une offre-famille?

Then change roles and ask and answer similar questions for the journey from Fréjus to Dieppe.

EXERCISE 7

With a partner, see how many questions you can ask and answer using the timetable below.

Numéro du train		5003	6933	1550/1	6941	6693	49	4564/5	6947	6949	1573/2	249	5051
Notes à consulter		22		23			24	25			26		27
Marseille-St-Charles	D	13.13		15.14			16.15	16.35	16.39		17.12		17.23
La Ciotat	D						16.44				17.38		
Bandol	D						16.56				17.50		
Toulon	D	13.55		15.59			17.34	17.18	17.23		18.05		18.11
Les Arcs	A			16.33			18.34						18.45
Fréjus	A												19.01
St-Raphael-Valescure	A	14.42		16.50			18.05	18.13		18.25	18.57		19.07
Cannes	A	15.08	15.00	17.14	17.07		18.29	18.37	18.50	19.03	19.24		19.32
Juan-les-Pins	A	15.19	15.09	17.25	17.16			18.48	19.00	19.20	19.35		19.43
Antibes	A	15.23	15.13	17.29	17.20		18.39	18.53	19.04	19.24	19.40		19.48
Cagnes-sur-Mer	A	15.32	15.24	17.38	17.31			19.02	19.16	19.36			19.57
Nice-Ville	A	15.43	15.39	17.50	17.46		18.55	19.13	19.31	19.51	20.00	20.17	20.07
Monaco-Monte-Carlo	A		16.11		18.23		19.12		19.57	20.17		20.31	20.45
Menton	A		16.25		18.38		19.22		20.10	20.30		20.41	20.56
Ventimiglia	A		16.37		18.54		19.35			20.42		20.54	21.10

22. CORAIL. 🛏.

23. CORAIL. 🛏 certains jours. ⊗. Jeune Voyageur Service.

24. Train à supplément sur le parcours étranger: les voyageurs en trafic international doivent etre munis du supplément avant l'accès au train. 🛏 certains jours.

25. Circule:du 27 juin au 7 sept 86 : tous les jours. CORAIL.

26. CORAIL. 🍽🛏. Jeune Voyageur Service.

27. CORAIL. ⊗🛏 certains jours. Jeune Voyageur Service.

28. CORAIL. ⊗.🛏. Jeune Voyageur Service.

Symboles

A	Arrivée
D	Départ
↤	Couchettes
🛏	Voitures-Lits
IC	Intercités
✕	Voiture restaurant
⊗	Grill-express
▭	Restauration à la place
♈	Bar
🛒	Vente ambulante

 ALLÔ! ALLÔ!

Which or what?

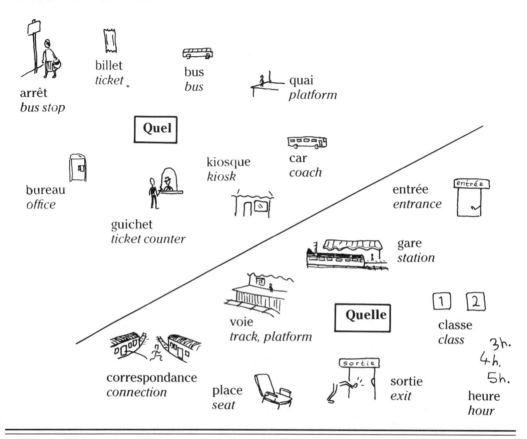

EXERCISE 8

With a partner, make 20 small cards on which are written the names below. Place these upside down on the table. The first player picks up one, and if it is, for example, a station, he says 'Il faut aller à quelle gare?'

The partner must guess which of the two station names is on the card, and say either:

Il faut aller à la gare du Nord *or*
Il faut aller à la gare Austerlitz.

If s/he guesses correctly, s/he wins the card. If not, the partner wins it. Names to write on the cards:

à la gare du Nord
à la gare Austerlitz
   au quai numéro 1
   au quai numéro 2
au guichet numéro 3
au guichet numéro 4
   à la sortie près du kiosque
   à la sortie près des toilettes
au bureau d'en face
au bureau près de la sortie

au kiosque de journaux
au kiosque là-bas
   à l'entrée à droite
   à l'entrée à gauche
   à la voie numéro 5
   à la voie numéro 6
   à l'arrêt numéro 7
   à l'arrêt numéro 8
à la place près de la fenêtre
à la place près du couloir

TRAVEL 47

Finding out where and when

Le train	part pour	Paris Nice	de quelle gare? de quelle voie?
Le bus Le tram		Boulogne Rouen	de quel arrêt? à quelle heure?

*Say as many sensible sentences as you can from this table. Remember, a bus can't leave from a **gare**, and a tram can't leave from a **voie**.*

EXERCISE 9

With a partner, take turns to ask these questions, and answer them by choosing a suitable reply from below:

la gare du Nord   2.00   no. 5   3.30   no. 2   no. 21   à gauche   à droite   la gare de l'Est

Pour aller à	Paris Nice Boulogne Rouen Evian Avignon Marseille Lyon	c'est quel (le)	train (*train*) s.v.p.? gare (*station*) voie (*platform*) arrêt (*bus stop*) guichet (*counter*) entrée (*entrance*) sortie (*exit*) vol (*flight*)

EXERCISE 10

You are an official at the enquiry office at the Air and Space Museum. With the help of the diagram below, try to answer a series of questions put to you by travellers.

1 Pour aller de la gare de l'Est au musée, c'est quel bus, s.v.p.?
2 Pour aller du musée à l'autoroute A1, c'est quelle sortie, s.v.p.?
3 Pour aller du boulevard périphérique jusqu'au musée, c'est quelle route, s.v.p.?
4 Où est-ce qu'on prend le bus no. 152? Et où est-ce qu'on descend?
5 Est-ce qu'il y a un parking au musée? Où ça?

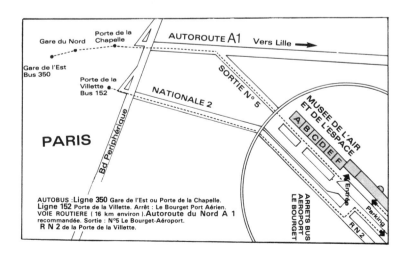

Travel by plane, bus or coach

Donnez-moi *Give me*	une deux trois	place(s)	Paris-Londres Paris-New York Paris-Tel Aviv	pour le	quatre cinq six	mai juin juillet	s'il vous plaît *please*

DONNEZ-MOI ... S'IL VOUS PLAÎT

EXERCISE 11 The above table provides you with 81 different sentences. See how many you can say in 1 minute.

The 24-hour clock

This is used for rail, road and air timetables to avoid confusion between morning and evening times.

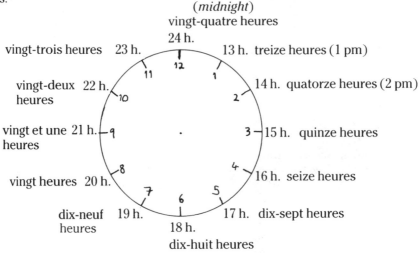

EXERCISE 12 Give the French for the following times, according to the 24-hour clock. E.g. 8.10pm – vingt heures dix.

1.05 pm	2.10 pm	3.15 pm	4.20 pm	5.25 pm	6.30 pm	7.35 pm

8.40 pm	9.45 pm	10.50 pm	1.55 pm	12.05 midnight.

EXERCISE 13 Choose a partner. One of you is the conductor in charge of the **bateau-mouche,** and the other is the traveller. Study the advertisement and you will be able to ask and answer all kinds of questions, e.g.

TRAVEL 49

Si on part à ... heures, on arrive à quelle heure? Quel est le prix de l'excursion?
Si on veut partir à 15h. 15, qu'est-ce qu'il faut faire?
Si on part à midi (14.30, 15.30, 20.30, 21h., dimanche à 13h) qu'est-ce qu'il y a comme prestations (special service)?
A quelle heure est-ce qu'on sert le déjeuner/goûter/dîner?
Quel est le prix du déjeuner/goûter/dîner?
Est-ce qu'on sert le déjeuner/goûter/dîner tous les jours?
Quels sont les numéros de téléphone pour les réservations?
Il faut descendre à quelle station de Métro?
Il faut prendre quel autobus?
Decrivez le programme de divertissements.

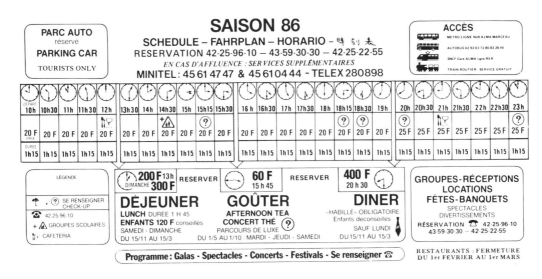

EXERCISE 14

Look at the various journeys possible between Paris and the Airport at Orly. With a partner, ask and answer questions such as:

Si on prend le bus d'Air France/l'Orlybus/le train/l'hélicoptere, où est-ce qu'on monte, si on part de (a) Paris, (b) Orly? Et où est-ce qu'on descend?
Il y a un bus/un train/un hélicoptère tous les combien?
Le trajet dure combien de temps?

Paris ⟷ Aéroport d'Orly

		Départ de Paris	Départ d'Orly**
AIR FRANCE	30 mn en moyenne entre Invalides et Orly* départ toutes les 12 mn	Aérogare des Invalides ou Gare Montparnasse (36, av. du Maine) de 5h50 à 23h	Orly Sud : porte J Orly Ouest : niveau Arrivée, porte E de 5h50 à 23h
		*Direct entre Paris-Montparnasse et Orly. **Direct entre Orly et Paris. Arrêt à la demande Pte d'Orléans et M° Duroc. Cars supplémentaires pour les arrivées d'avions après 23h30.	
	25 mn en moyenne entre Denfert-Rochereau et Orly départ toutes les 15 mn	Place Denfert-Rochereau (devant la gare RER) Hôtel PLM St-Jacques de 6h05 à 23h	Orly Sud : porte F de 6h32 à 23h30 Orly Ouest : niveau Arrivée porte D de 6h34 à 23h32

50 ALLÔ! ALLÔ!

		Départ de Paris	Départ d'Orly
35 mn entre Austerlitz et Orly départ toutes les 15 mn*		Gares (RER)(C) Bd Victor, Javel, Champ de Mars, Pont de l'Alma, Invalides, Quai d'Orsay, Pont St-Michel, Austerlitz, Bd Masséna. Austerlitz : de 5 h 50 à 22 h 50	Orly Sud : porte H de 5 h 31 à 23 h 15 Orly Ouest : niveau Arrivée porte F de 5 h 38 à 23 h 23

*Départ supplémentaire à 5 h 20. Le soir, départ toutes les 30 mn

		Départ de Paris	Départ d'Orly
6 mn entre Héliport de Paris et Orly départ toutes les heures		Héliport de Paris* 4, av. de la Porte-de-Sèvres Paris 15ᵉ toutes les heures de 8 h 16 à 19 h 16 sauf 13 h 16 et 15 h 16	Orly Sud : 1ᵉʳ étage, salle 3 Orly Ouest : niveau départ, Hall 2 toutes les heures de 8 h 30 à 19 h 30 sauf 13 h 30 et 15 h 30

* Renseignements et réservation : tél. 554.95.11

l'aérogare
the air terminal

l'autobus
the bus

le car
the coach

Où se trouve . . . ?
Where is . . . ?

l'aéroport
the airport

la gare routière
the bus station

l'arrêt d'autobus
the bus stop

l'avion
the aeroplane

le terminus
the terminus

EXERCISE Can you ask where the following things or places are?

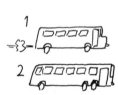 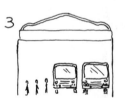  

(15) Give an answer from one of the following:
là-bas à gauche/là-bas à droite/là-bas – allez tout droit/il faut prendre un bus/il faut trouver arrêt no. 63.

EXERCISE (16) Revision. What would you say in the following situations?
1 You want to buy a single ticket to Lourdes.   2 You want to buy a return ticket to Lyons.   3 You want to buy a book of tickets for the Métro.   4 You can't work out which ligne you must take on the Métro.   5 You want to know where the exit is.   6 You don't know whether you have to change trains or not.   7 Tell somebody that smoking is

TRAVEL 51

forbidden. **8** *You don't know which platform to go to for your train.* **9** *You want to buy two tickets, tourist class, Paris to London.* **10** *You need to know if the train leaves at 6 pm.* **11** *You want to know if a seat is taken.* **12** *You wish to apologise.* **13** *You don't know where the bus stop is.* **14** *You need to know how often the buses run.* **15** *You would like to know if you can reserve a seat in the train which leaves at 10 o'clock for Boulogne.*

EXERCISE 17

Rôle-playing.
1 *You are in a bus station in Paris, and want to make a day trip to Chartres to see the cathedral. Make enquiries about the time of the coaches and the price, and book return tickets for yourself and your friend. Your partner can be the booking clerk.*
2 *You are at Toulouse airport, and wish to book a flight to London for yourself in a week's time. Ask about the time and price, reserve a place and buy a ticket. Your partner can be the counter clerk.*

CONVERSATION 1 ● Booking a ticket

Un billet pour Calais, s.v.p.	*A ticket for Calais, please.*
Single or return?	Un aller simple ou un aller-retour?
Un aller-retour, s.v.p.	*A return, please.*
1st class or 2nd class?	Première classe ou seconde classe?
Seconde classe, s.v.p. Je vous dois combien?	*2nd class, please. How much is that?*
200 francs please.	Deux cents francs, s.v.p.
Le train part à quelle heure?	*What time does the train leave?*
At 2 pm.	A quatorze heures.
Est-ce qu'il faut changer?	*Do I have to change?*
No, it's a through train.	Non, c'est un train direct.
Le trajet dure combien de temps?	*How long does it take?*
2 hours.	Deux heures.
Le train part de quelle voie?	*What platform does the train leave from?*

From platform 10, m . . . — De la voie numéro dix, m . . .

Excusez-moi, c'est bien le train pour Calais, s.v.p.? — *Excuse me, is this the right train for Calais, please?*

Yes, that's right. — Oui, c'est ça.

Est-ce que cette place est libre? — *Is this seat free?*

No, it's taken. It's reserved. — Non, c'est occupé. C'est réservé.

Oh, je m'excuse. — *Oh, I'm sorry.*

Don't mention it, m . . . — Je vous en prie, m . . .

CONVERSATION 2 • Travel by bus

Est-ce qu'il y a un bus ou un car pour Nantes demain, s.v.p.? — *Is there a bus or a coach for Nantes tomorrow, please?*

There's a coach at 3 p.m. — Il y a un car à quinze heures.

Je voudrais réserver deux places, deux allers (simples), s.v.p. — *I want to book two seats, two singles, please.*

There you are, m . . . That's 100 francs. — Voilà, m . . . Ça fait cent francs, s.v.p.

Voilà. On arrive à Nantes à quelle heure? — *There you are. When do we arrive at Nantes?*

At 6 pm. — A dix-huit heures.

Où est-ce qu'on prend le car? — *Where do we get on the coach?*

At the bus station – and you get off at the town hall at Nantes. — A la gare routière – et (à Nantes) on descend à la mairie.

La gare routière est près d'ici? — *Is the bus station near here?*

No. You'll have to get a bus. — Non. Il faut prendre un bus.

Il y a un bus tous les combien? — *How often is there a bus?*

Every 20 minutes. — Toutes les vingt minutes.

Où se trouve l'arrêt? — *Where's the bus stop?*

Over there, m . . . — Là-bas, m . . .

Merci beaucoup, m . . . — *Thank you very much, m . . .*

TRAVEL 53

CONVERSATION 3 • Informing someone of your arrival time

Bonjour! Est-ce que M. Susse est là, s.v.p.?

Who's speaking?

C'est de la part de Martin.

Ah, Martin! How are you? It's Michael speaking.

Très bien, merci. Je téléphone pour te dire l'heure de mon arrivée.

Oh yes. It's tomorrow, isn't it?

Oui. Je compte quitter Paris à 10 heures, et arriver à la gare de Soissons à 11.15.

Good. We'll come and meet you. See you tomorrow. Have a good journey! Goodbye!

Hello! Is M. Susse there, please?

C'est de la part de qui?

It's Martin.

Ah, Martin! Comment vas-tu? C'est Michel à l'appareil.

Very well, thanks. I'm phoning to tell you my arrival time.

Ah oui. C'est demain, n'est-ce pas?

Yes. I'm expecting to leave Paris at 10 o'clock and arrive at the station at Soissons at 11.15.

Bon. On ira te chercher. A demain. Bon voyage! Au revoir!

5. Arranging to meet someone

Responses

If you would like to accept the invitation, say:
  Oui, je veux bien, merci.
If you don't want to go, or cannot, say:
  Je regrette, je ne peux pas y aller (aujourd'hui). *I'm sorry, I can't go (today).*
  Si on y allait demain? *How about going tomorrow?*
or
  Je ne veux pas y aller. *I don't want to go there.*
  Si on allait au...? *How about going to the...?*

EXERCISE

Can you give a suitable reply to the following invitations?

1 Veux-tu aller au cinéma avec moi ce soir? (*Yes*).
2 Veux-tu aller au théâtre avec moi ce soir? (*Not the theatre. Suggest the cinema.*)
3 Veux-tu venir au café avec moi ce soir? (*You can't today. Suggest tomorrow.*)
4 Veux-tu venir à la piscine avec moi? (*You can't today. Suggest Tuesday.*)
5 Veux-tu aller à la disco avec moi? (*Not the disco. Suggest the football match.*)
6 Veux-tu aller au marché avec Marie? (*Not with Marie. Suggest going with Bernadette.*)
7 Tu connais Georges? Veux-tu aller au stade avec lui? (*Not with Georges. Suggest going with Charles.*)

MEETING SOMEONE

8 Tu connais Sébastien? Veux-tu aller au restaurant avec lui? (*Not the restaurant. Suggest the café.*)
9 Tu connais Isabelle? Veux-tu aller au club avec elle? (*Yes. Suggest going tomorrow.*)
10 Tu connais Nicholas? Veux-tu aller au match avec lui? (*You can't go today. Suggest next Saturday.*)

Your partner invites you to one of the outings suggested on the previous page, along with another boy or girl. Close your eyes, point at random to one of the circles below, and respond accordingly.

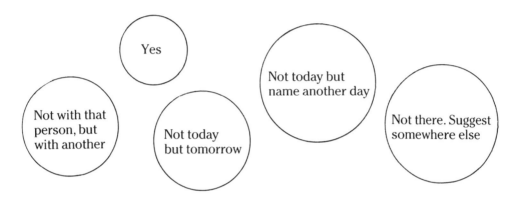

Make 11 cards illustrating the places shown in the diagram at the beginning of the lesson. Show them one by one to your partner. S/he must ask 'Veux-tu aller ... avec moi/lui/elle?', according to the picture on the card. You must give any suitable reply.

Where to meet

devant	*in front of*
derrière	*behind*
en face du/de la	*opposite*
près du/de la	*near*

You have met a new friend, and you are arranging a 'date' with him or her. However, your new date is not a very obliging person, and each time you suggest a meeting place and time, s/he suggests a different one.
  What are the suggestions made by your date in answer to your ideas? E.g.
  Si on se rencontrait devant le cinéma à une heure et demie?
  Response: Ah, non! Je préfère devant le café à deux heures.

1 Si on se rencontrait derrière le club à deux heures?
2 Si on se rencontrait près du cinéma à deux heures et demie?
3 Si on se rencontrait en face du stade à trois heures?

56 ALLÔ! ALLÔ!

4 Si on se rencontrait devant la piscine à quatre heures et quart?
5 Si on se rencontrait près du restaurant à huit heures?
6 Si on se rencontrait derrière le marché à midi?
7 Si on se rencontrait devant la disco à six heures?
8 Si on se rencontrait devant la gare à sept heures et quart?
9 Si on se rencontrait dans le bar à huit heures moins le quart?
10 Si on se rencontrait en face du club à neuf heures?

EXERCISE 5

Rôle-playing.

1 *You and your friend are looking at these advertisements and trying to decide which entertainment to go to. Suggest each one in turn ('Si on allait . . .') and try to persuade your friend by praising it. Each time your friend is unwilling to go, so you have to suggest the next advertisement.*

33 CLUNY PALACE
GREYSTOKE
La légende de Tarzan
ADIEU BONAPARTE v.o.

45 SAINT-MICHEL
DELIVRANCE
2001 L'ODYSSEE DE L'ESPACE

MEETING SOMEONE 57

2 Ring up a few of your friends (their parts are taken in turn by your partner) and invite each one to a different social event or outing. Some agree to come, and some don't. If they don't they must give a reason why.
3 Ring up a friend (played by your partner) and try to arrange a party. Your friend objects to the first few people you want to invite, and says why. Finally you agree on which friends to invite, when to hold the party and where.

Useful vocabulary

il/elle est moche	s/he's awful/ghastly
il/elle est trop sérieux (-euse)	s/he's too serious
il/elle est égoïste	s/he's selfish
il/elle est trop vantarde	s/he's too boastful

CONVERSATION 1 ● Arranging to meet someone

Allô! C'est Marie? C'est Paul à l'appareil.	Hello! Is that Marie? This is Paul speaking.
Oh, hello, Paul. How're things?	Ah, bonjour, Paul. Comment ça va?
Très bien, merci. Dis donc, veux-tu aller au cinéma demain?	Very well, thanks. I say, would you like to go to the pictures tomorrow?
What's on?	Qu'est-ce qu'on joue?
C'est 'Super-jazz'	It's 'Super-jazz'

ALLÔ! ALLÔ!

Yes, I'd like to, thanks. Where shall we meet?

Si on se retrouvait en face du cinéma à sept heures moins le quart? C'est possible?

Oh no, that's a bit too early. Seven o'clock's better.

Bon. D'accord. A tout à l'heure.

(LATER)

Goodness! It's half past seven! Where is she?

Oh, I'm sorry, Paul. I'm late, I know. I missed the bus.

Ah, ça ne fait rien. Entrons.

Oui, je veux bien, merci. Où est-ce qu'on se retrouve?

How about meeting opposite the cinema at 6.45? Is that possible?

Ah, non, c'est un peu trop tôt. Sept heures, c'est mieux.

Fine. O.K. See you later.

Mince! Il est sept heures et demie! Où est-elle?

Ah, je m'excuse, Paul. Je suis en retard, je sais. J'ai manqué le bus.

Oh, it doesn't matter. Let's go in.

6) At a post office or bank, at the Customs desk

aller au guichet
go to the counter

envoyer une lettre
send a telegram

envoyer un colis
send a parcel

changer (toucher) un chèque de voyage
change (cash) a traveller's cheque

envoyer un mandat postal
send a postal order

Il faut
I have to

envoyer une carte postale
send a post card

trouver mon passe-port
find my passport

remplir une formule
fill in a form
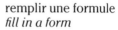

acheter des timbres
buy some stamps

téléphoner
'phone

trouver un jeton
find a 'jeton' (for the 'phone)

trouver la cabine téléphonique
find the 'phone booth

trouver l'annuaire
find the directory

EXERCISE 1

Using the vocabulary above, complete the following sentences:

1 Il faut

2 Il faut

3 Est-ce qu'il faut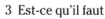

4 Est-ce qu'il faut

5 Il faut

60 ALLÔ! ALLÔ!

6 Il faut

7 Il faut

8 Il n'est pas nécessaire de

9 Il n'est pas nécessaire de

10 Il n'est pas nécessaire de

EXERCISE 2

Consequences. Your partner states each of the following situations in turn, and you must tell him/her what to do. The vocabulary in Exercise 1 will help you. Start your replies with 'Il faut . . .' E.g.

Je veux téléphoner à mon copain.
Answer: Eh bien, il faut trouver l'annuaire.

1 C'est l'anniversaire de maman la semaine prochaine.
2 J'ai manqué mon train, et mon oncle m'attend!
3 Ma moto est tombée en panne!
4 J'ai oublié le numéro de téléphone de Jean.
5 Je veux changer un chèque de voyage.
6 Je dois acheter des timbres.
7 Je veux remplir un formulaire.
8 Je dois envoyer un colis à ma tante.
9 Je dois acheter des souvenirs pour ma famille.
10 Je dois téléphoner tout de suite.

EXERCISE 3

Revision of **Est-ce que je peux . . .?, Où est-ce que je peux . . .?, C'est combien?, Quel (le) . . .?**

1 *Ask if you can buy some stamps here.* **2** *Ask if you can change a traveller's cheque here.* **3** *Ask where you can find a directory.* **4** *Ask where you can find the phone booth.* **5** *Ask how much it is to telephone to Paris.* **6** *Ask how much it is to send a parcel to England.* **7** *Ask how much it is to send a postcard to Madrid.* **8** *Ask which form it is.* **9** *Ask which counter it is.* **10** *Ask which directory it is.*

JE CHERCHE

Je cherche	un tabac la poste une boîte à lettres	a tobacconist's the post office a letter box	s.v.p.?

POST OFFICE, BANK, CUSTOMS

EXERCISE 4a

Ask how much it costs to send the following articles to the countries stated. Your partner can give a suitable reply. Then you must ask for either a post office, a letter box or a tobacconist's and your partner can give you instructions as to how to reach it.
Start by saying 'Je veux envoyer ...

What?	Where to?	How much?	Where are you going?
une lettre	England	?	post office
un colis	Spain	?	tobacconist's
une carte-postale	Germany	?	letter box
un mandat postal	U.S.A.	?	post office

Donnez-moi	1 timbre(s) à 2 3 4	10 francs 20 centimes 30 40	s.v.p.

Say as many sentences in one minute as you can from the above table.

EXERCISE 4b

Allô! Allô! *A telephone game.* Make 10 to 20 small cards, each containing either a picture (of a cinema, hotel, garage, football, etc.) or a simple message such as 'Tell him/her you can't come' 'Tell him/her it'll be 3.30'.

Imagine you have rung up your partner. You begin by saying to one another the first four sentences of Conversation 2 ('In the phone booth') from page 62. Then the one who has answered the phone picks up one of the cards at random, and the one who is making the call must immediately make up a message which has some reference to the picture. The partner should try to ask a few questions about the message.

You can exchange your set of cards with someone else's if you would like a few surprises!

EXERCISE 5

Rôle playing.
1 Imagine you are Paul in Conversation 2 on page 62. Ring back Renée and have the conversation which you couldn't have an hour previously. You wanted to tell her that your motor-bike has broken down, and you can't get to her house today, as expected. You hope to arrive tomorrow.
2 You are in a French post office with a newcomer from England who wants to post some letters and postcards, buy some stamps, send a parcel and phone someone, but doesn't know what to do, and asks you for advice.

CONVERSATION 1 ● At the post office

Bonjour, m ... Je voudrais acheter des timbres, s.v.p. C'est combien pour envoyer une carte-postale en Angleterre?	*Good morning/afternoon, m ... I'd like to buy some stamps, please. How much is it to send a postcard to England?*
2 francs, please.	Deux francs, s.v.p.

62 ALLÔ! ALLÔ!

Alors, donnez-moi deux timbres à deux francs, s.v.p.

Then give me 2 stamps at 2 francs, please.

There you are, m . . .

Voilà, m . . .

Merci. Je voudrais aussi un jeton pour la cabine téléphonique, s.v.p. et l'annuaire.

Thank you. I'd also like a jeton for the phone booth, please – and the directory.

There you are. Is that all?

Voilà. C'est tout?

Oui, c'est tout, merci.

Yes, that's all, thank you.

CONVERSATION 2 ● In the 'phone booth

Allô! Est-ce que Madame Lenoir est là, s.v.p.?

Hello! Is Madame Lenoir there, please?

Who's speaking?

C'est de la part de qui?

C'est de la part de Paul Delain.

It's Paul Delain speaking.

Righto! Hold the line . . .
 New voice: Hello! Renée Lenoir speaking.

Ah bon! Ne quittez pas . . .
 New voice: Allô! Renée Lenoir à l'appareil.

Bonjour, madame. C'est Paul.

Hello, madame. It's Paul.

Oh hello, Paul! –but, will you call later? I'm very busy just now – I have visitors.

Ah bonjour, Paul! Mais . . veux-tu rappeler plus tard? Je suis très occupée en ce moment – j'ai des invités.

D'accord. Je rappellerai dans une heure. A tout à l'heure!

O.K. I'll call back in an hour. Cheerio!

POST OFFICE, BANK, CUSTOMS

CONVERSATION 3 — At the Customs desk

Vous vous appelez comment?
What's your name?

My name's . . .
Je m'appelle . . .

Vous êtes de quelle nationalité?
What nationality are you?

I'm English.
Anglais(e).

Quel âge avez-vous?
How old are you?

I'm 15.
J'ai quinze ans.

Quelle est votre adresse?
What's your address?

30, MacDonald Street, Ramsgate.
30 MacDonald Street, Ramsgate.

Montrez-moi vos bagages, s.v.p.
Show me your luggage, please.

Here they are.
Les voici.

Qu'est-ce que vous avez acheté en France?
What have you bought in France?

I've bought a film, a bottle of plonk, and some souvenirs.
J'ai acheté une pellicule, une bouteille de rouge, et des souvenirs.

Vous n'avez rien à déclarer?
Haven't you anything to declare?

Yes. I've bought a watch. Here it is.
Si. J'ai acheté une montre. La voici.

Où l'avez-vous achetée?
Where did you buy it?

At the 'Printemps', in Paris.
Au 'Printemps' à Paris.

Quand l'avez-vous achetée?
When did you buy it?

Last week – July 24.
La semaine dernière – le 24 juillet.

Elle a coûté combien?
How much did it cost?

£30.
300 francs.

Je regrette, il faut payer les droits de douane. Ce n'est pas exonéré.
I'm sorry, you'll have to pay duty. It's not duty-free.

Too bad!
Tant pis!

CONVERSATION 4 • At an exchange bureau or bank

Je cherche un bureau de change s.v.p.? – Ah, c'est par ici . . .

Where is there an exchange bureau, please? Ah, it's here . . .

Bonjour, m . . . Je voudrais toucher deux chèques de voyage, s.v.p. Est-ce qu'il faut remplir un formulaire?

Good morning, m . . . I'd like to cash two traveller's cheques, please. Must I fill in a form?

No. It's not necessary. Have you got your passport, please?

Non. Ce n'est pas nécessaire. Vous avez votre passeport, s.v.p.?

Oui, m . . . Le voici.

Yes. Here it is.

How much do you want?

Vous voulez combien?

Je voudrais toucher deux chèques de 100 francs, s.v.p., m . . .

I'd like to cash two cheques of 100 francs, please.

Will you sign here, please? Thank you. Now you must go to the cash desk.

Voulez-vous signer ici, s.v.p.? Merci. Maintenant il faut aller à la caisse.

(A la caisse)

(At the cash desk)

Deux chèques de cent francs – vous voulez l'argent comment?

Two cheques of 100 francs each – how do you want the money?

150 francs in 50-franc notes, and the rest in small change, please.

Cent cinquante francs en billets de cinquante francs, et le reste en petite monnaie, s.v.p., m . . .

Bon. Voilà. Au revoir, et merci.

Right. There you are. Goodbye, and thank you.

Goodbye, m . . . Thank you.

Au revoir, m . . . Merci.

At a café or restaurant

EXERCISE 1

A Game – 'Happy Menus'. This is another variation of the old 'Happy Families' game. You need to make 4 cards for each part of the menu, as described on page 00 for the 'Happy Tomatoes' game. The rules of the game are the same.

Here are some suggestions for the 'families' you can make:

charcuterie:	salami	jambon	pâté de foie	bacon
cold meats:	*salami*	*ham*	*liver pâté*	*bacon*
fruits de mer:	crabe	moule	langoustine	huître
seafood:	*crab*	*mussel*	*prawn*	*oyster*
poissons:	thon	truite	morue	maquereau
fish:	*tuna*	*trout*	*cod*	*mackerel*
viande:	bifteck garni	steak haché	côtelettes	veau
meat:	*steak*	*beefburger*	*cutlets*	*veal*
omelettes:	au jambon	au fromage	aux tomates	aux fines herbes
omelettes:	*ham*	*cheese*	*tomato*	*with herbs*
légumes:	frites	purée de pommes de terre	haricots verts	chou-fleur
vegetables:	*chips*	*mashed potatoes*	*green beans*	*cauliflower*
fruits:	poire	ananas	pamplemousse	prunes
fruit:	*pear*	*pineapple*	*grapefruit*	*plums*
desserts:	tarte aux pommes	pâtisseries	yaourt	tarte aux cerises
dessert:	*apple tart*	*cakes*	*yoghurt*	*cherry tart*
glaces:	à la vanille	au chocolat	à la fraise	à la framboise
ice cream:	*vanilla*	*chocolate*	*strawberry*	*raspberry*
fromages:	Camembert	Brie	Roquefort	Bleu
cheese:	*Camembert*	*Brie*	*Roquefort*	*Blue*
vin:	vin rouge	vin blanc	vin rosé	vin de table
wine:	*red wine*	*white wine*	*rosé wine*	*table wine*
boissons:	coca	orangina	limonade	lait
drinks:	*coca-cola*	*orangeade*	*lemonade*	*milk*
boissons chaudes	thé	chocolat	café noir	café crème
hot drinks:	*tea*	*hot chocolate*	*black coffee*	*coffee with cream*

EXERCISE 2

The game of pairs. Make a set of about 40 squares of paper or card and play the game of pairs described in lesson 3 on page 27, using the words given for 'Happy Menus' in Exercise 1.

Ordering drinks

une bière — *a beer*
un coca-cola — *coca cola*
un jus d'orange — *orange juice*
une limonade — *lemonade*
un café crème — *coffee with cream*
un café noir — *black coffee*
un jus d'ananas — *pineapple juice*
un thé au citron — *tea with lemon*
un verre de vin blanc — *a glass of white wine*
un verre de vin rouge — *a glass of red wine*
un jus de pamplemousse — *grapefruit juice*
un thé au lait — *tea with milk*
un verre de lait — *a glass of milk*

Je voudrais *I'd like*
Avez-vous? *Have you?*
S'il vous plaît *please*

EXERCISE

For this you need a partner. One of you takes the part of a waiter or waitress in a café, and the other is the customer. The customer enters the café, and asks what is available in the way of sandwiches and drinks. The waiter replies, and the customer orders.

If you prefer, more than two can take part, with one waiter and several customers.

Ordering desserts

The following are some of the mouth-watering desserts you may be offered in a French restaurant:

tarte aux pommes	*apple tart*
tarte aux cerises	*cherry tart*
tarte aux fraises	*strawberry tart*
fraises à la crème	*strawberries and cream*
framboises à la crème	*raspberries and cream*
glace à la vanille	*vanilla ice*
glace au citron	*lemon ice*
glace au chocolat	*chocolate ice*
pêche melba	*peaches with ice-cream*

AT A CAFE OR RESTAURANT 67

FRUITS:	FRUIT:
pommes	apples
poires	pears
prunes	plums
bananes	bananas
oranges	oranges
ananas	pineapple
pamplemousse	grapefruit

pâtisseries	fancy cakes
fromage	cheese
yaourt	yogurt

EXERCISE 4 Can you write out the following menus in French?

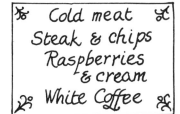

Cold meat
Steak & chips
Raspberries & cream
White Coffee

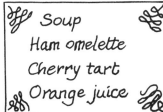

Soup
Ham omelette
Cherry tart
Orange juice

Soup
Plain omelette
Vanilla ice
Black coffee

Salad
Beefburger
Apple tart
Red wine

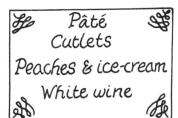

Pâté
Cutlets
Peaches & ice-cream
White wine

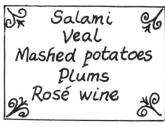

Salami
Veal
Mashed potatoes
Plums
Rosé wine

EXERCISE 5 'Et pour suivre, je prends ...' The first person in the game must name a food or drink beginning with the letter 'a'. The next person repeats the word, adding a word starting with 'b'. The third person will say three words, and so on. Go through the alphabet. If you make a mistake, you are out. It would be more fun to play this game in groups of five or six than with the whole class at once.

EXERCISE 6 Now you are ready to order a full-scale meal. Take parts as waiter/waitress and customer(s) as you did for exercise 3. This time you are ordering a full meal. You can base it on the menu illustrated overleaf. Now and again ask the waiter/waitress to explain what a dish is made of, by saying:

Qu'est-ce que c'est que la soupe de campagne à l'ancienne?
                les écrevisses   ?
                la princesse champagne   ?   etc.

 ALLÔ! ALLÔ!

MENU 27 F   1/2 VIN COMPRIS

Sauf Samedi et Dimanche :
SOUPE DE CAMPAGNE A L'ANCIENNE
CHARCUTERIE
PLAT DU JOUR
DESSERT

MENU
à 42 F
1/2 ROUGE COMPRIS

SOUPE DE CAMPAGNE A L'ANCIENNE
°
CHARCUTERIE
°
MAGRET DE CANARD FRAIS (2 personnes)
ou
COTE DE BŒUF A L'OS (2 personnes)
ou
CŒURS D'OIE ET CANARD FRAIS
ou
AGNEAUX DE MONTAGNE
le tout garni
°
FROMAGES ou FRUITS ou GLACES

SPECIALITES :   SUPPLEMENT 5 F

DESSERTS :
    MYSTERES
    PRINCESSE CHAMPAGNE
    FROMAGE DE CHEVRE
    D'ESCANECRABE
    CROUSTADES

NOS GRILLADES SONT UNIQUEMENT FAITES
AU FEU DE BOIS

MENU
à 48 F
1/2 ROUGE COMPRIS

SOUPE DE CAMPAGNE A L'ANCIENNE
°
PATE DE CAMPAGNE
JAMBONNEAU NATUREL
SAUCISSON DE CAMPAGNE
°
MAGRET DE CANARD FRAIS (2 personnes)
ou
COTE DE BŒUF A L'OS (2 personnes)
ou
CŒURS D'OIE ET CANARD FRAIS
ou
AGNEAUX DE MONTAGNE
le tout garni
°
FROMAGES ou FRUITS ou GLACES

SPECIALITES :   SUPPLEMENT 5 F

DESSERTS :
    MYSTERES
    PRINCESSE CHAMPAGNE
    FROMAGE DE CHEVRE
    D'ESCANECRABE
    CROUSTADES

SPECIALITES :	
FOIE GRAS ENTIER AU NATUREL	30,00 F
CONFIT FROID AU NATUREL	20,00 F
ECREVISSES A L'AMERICAINE	25,00 F
PALOMBES ou PIGEONS aux CEPES	25,00 F

Pour finir votre soirée, **LA GUINGUETTE** vous
attend à Boulogne   Tél. 88.21.67

EXERCISE 7

What do you think each of the following would order to eat and drink in a café? Give 4 items for each person.

AT A CAFE OR RESTAURANT

Paying

Some useful phrases:

Apportez-moi l'addition, s'il vous plaît.	*Bring me the bill, please.*
Est-ce que le service est compris?	*Is the service included?*
Non, ce n'est pas compris.	*No, it isn't included.*
Avez-vous de la monnaie?	*Have you any change?*
Excusez-moi, il y a erreur.	*Excuse me, there's a mistake.*
On a pris ... commandé ...	*We had ... ordered ...*
Mais on n'a pas pris ... commandé ...	*But we didn't have ... order ...*
Vous avez tort.	*You are wrong.*
Vous avez raison.	*You are right.*

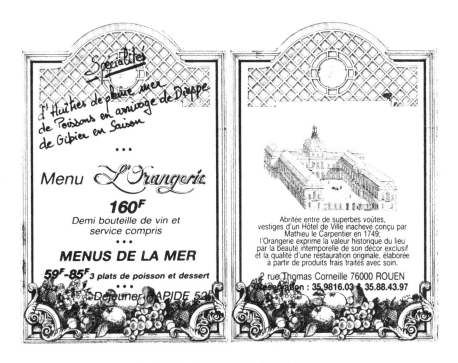

Rôle playing

1 *You are in a café, ordering sandwiches or light snacks, and drinks. Unfortunately, there isn't a very wide choice available in this café. Each time that you order something, the waiter says 'Je regrette, monsieur/mademoiselle, il n'y a pas de ... aujourd'hui,' so that you have to order something else. You are ordering for three people.*
2 *You are in a café with a friend. The waiter confuses your order with someone else's, and brings the wrong food. Tell him what you did not order, and what you did order.*
3 *You have just received the bill in a restaurant. You find four mistakes, either in the dishes you are supposed to have ordered, or in the prices charged. Explain to the waiter what is wrong with the bill.*
4 *You are in a café with your rather awkward young brother or sister. Each time you offer him/her something from the menu, s/he replies: 'Je n'aime pas ...' or 'Je ne veux pas de ...' Then s/he says 'Je veux ...'*

ALLÔ! ALLÔ!

CONVERSATION 1 — Ordering sandwiches

(GARÇON) Bonsoir, monsieur. Vous avez choisi?

(WAITER) Good evening, sir. Have you chosen?

(M. LEBRUN) What sort of sandwiches have you, please?

(M. LEBRUN) Qu'est-ce que vous avez comme sandwiches, s'il vous plaît?

(GARÇON) Nous avons jambon, pâté, fromage et tomates, monsieur.

(WAITER) Ham, pâté, cheese and tomato, sir.

(M.L.) Well, what would you like?

(M.L.) Eh bien, qu'est-ce que vous prenez?

(MME. L) Je prends un sandwich au jambon, s.v.p.

(MME. L) I'll have a ham sandwich, please.

(NICOLAS) I'll have a pâté sandwich, please.

(NICOLAS) Je prends un sandwich au pâté, s.v.p.

(LOUISE) Donnez-moi un sandwich au fromage, s.v.p.

(LOUISE) Give me a cheese sandwich, please.

(M.L.) Give me a tomato sandwich, please.

(M.L.) Donnez-moi un sandwich aux tomates, s.v.p.

(GARÇON) C'est tout, monsieur?

(WAITER) Is that all, sir?

(M.L.) No. We'd like four white coffees, please.

(M.L.) Non. Nous voulons aussi quatre crèmes, s.v.p.

(GARÇON) Très bien, monsieur. Merci.

(WAITER) Very good, sir. Thank you.

CONVERSATION 2 — Ordering the main meal

(M. LEBRUN) Y a-t-il une table de libre, s.v.p.? Nous sommes trois.

(M. LEBRUN) Is there a table available, please? There are three of us.

(WAITER) Yes, sir. Follow me, please.

(GARCON) Oui, monsieur. Suivez-moi, s.v.p.

(M.L.) Voudriez-vous m'apporter le menu, s.v.p.

(M.L.) Bring me the menu, please.

*(WAITER) Certainly, sir.
(5 minutes later . . .)
Have you chosen?*

(GARCON) Certainement, monsieur.
(5 minutes plus tard . . .)
Vous avez choisi?

(M.L.) Oui. On prend le menu à trente francs, s.v.p.

(M.L.) Yes. We'll have the 30-franc menu, please.

(WAITER) Very good, sir. What would you like to begin with?

(GARCON) Bien, monsieur. Que voulez-vous pour commencer?

(M.L.) Je prends la charcuterie, s.v.p.

(M.L.) I'll have the cold meat, please.

(MME. L.) *The salad, please.*

(MME. L.) La salade, s.v.p.

(NICOLAS) Le potage, s.v.p.

(NICOLAS) The soup, please.

(WAITER) And for the main course?

(GARCON) Et comme plat principal?

AT A CAFE OR RESTAURANT

(M.L.) Je prends le plat du jour, s.v.p.	*(M.L.) I'll have today's special, please.*
(MME. L.) I'll have a mushroom omelette and green beans, please.	(MME. L.) Je prends une omelette aux champignons et des haricots verts, s.v.p.
(NICOLAS) Je prends une omelette au jambon et des frites, s.v.p.	*(NICOLAS) I'll have a ham omelette and chips, please.*
(WAITER) And what would you like to drink?	(GARCON) Et comme boisson?
(M.L.) Une bière et trois limonades, s.v.p.	*(M.L.) A beer and three lemonades, please.*
(WAITER) Very good, sir. Thank you.	(GARCON) Très bien, monsieur. Merci.

CONVERSATION 3 ● Checking the bill

Monsieur! Voulez-vous apporter l'addition, s.v.p.?	*Waiter! Will you bring the bill, please?*
Certainly, sir. Here it is.	Certainement, monsieur. La voici.
Merci... Excusez-moi, il y a erreur.	*Thank you... Excuse me, there's a mistake.*
I'm sorry but I think you are mistaken.	Je regrette mais je crois que vous avez tort.
Non, j'ai raison. Regardez. On a pris le menu à prix fixe, n'est-ce pas?	*No, I'm right. Look. We had the fixed-price meal, didn't we?*
Yes, sir.	Oui, monsieur.
C'est combien, ce menu-là?	*How much is that menu?*
30 francs	Trente francs.
Nous sommes quatre. Alors, quatre fois trente francs, ça fait cent vingt francs.	*There are four of us. So, four times 30 francs is 120 francs.*
That's right.	C'est ça.
On a pris aussi quatre express. Quatre fois trois francs, ça fait douze francs.	*Besides that we had four espressos. Four times 3 francs is 12 francs.*
That's right.	C'est ça.
Mais on n'a pas commandé de vin.	*But we didn't order wine.*

Yes, that's true.	Oui, c'est exact.
Vous avez mis 'Une bouteille de vin blanc, vingt francs.'	*You have put 'One bottle of white wine, 20 francs.'*
Goodness. Is that so?	Ça alors! C'est vrai?
Est-ce que le service est compris?	*Is service included?*
Oh yes, sir. Service is included.	Mais oui, monsieur. Le service est compris.
Mais vous avez mis 'Service dix francs.'	*But you have put 'Service 10 francs'*
Goodness! Is that so?	Ça alors! C'est vrai?
Eh bien: pour le menu à prix fixe, cent vingt francs.	*Right: for the fixed-price menu, 120 francs.*
Yes, sir.	Oui, monsieur.
Pour le café, douze francs. Ça fait cent trente-deux francs en tout, non pas cent soixante-deux francs.	*For the coffee, 12 francs. That's 132 francs in all, not 162 francs.*
I'm sorry sir.	Je suis désolé, monsieur.
Ça ne fait rien . . . Le repas était delicieux – le fromage était parfait – mais l'addition ne l'était pas! Où est-ce qu'on paie?	*Don't mention it . . . The meal was delicious – the cheese was just right – but the bill wasn't! Where do we pay?*

8 Lost property, repairs

What have you lost?

mes chèques de voyage
my traveller's cheques

mon appareil
my camera

mon argent
my money

mes lunettes de soleil
my sunglasses

ma valise
my suitcase

J'ai Perdu
I have lost

mon passe-port
my passport

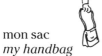
mon sac
my handbag

mon porte-monnaie
my purse

mon porte-feuille
my wallet

What is it like?

petit
small

nouveau
new

blanc
white

noir
black

en argent
silver

C'est
It's

en or
gold

vieux
old

grand
large

bleu
blue

en plastique
plastic

en cuir
leather

*If the article you have lost is in the plural, e.g. sunglasses or traveller's cheques, begin your description by saying **Ils/Elles sont** . . . If you are writing the description, most adjectives*

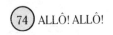 ALLÔ! ALLÔ!

should have an extra 's' added to them in the plural, e.g.

Enquirer: J'ai perdu mes lunettes de soleil.
Clerk: Elles sont comment?
Enquirer: Elles sont noires ... vieilles ... en plastique.
Clerk: Est-ce que votre nom est marqué dessus?
Enquirer: Malheureusement, non! Mon nom n'est pas marqué dessus.

EXERCISE *With the following pictures as a guide, tell an assistant at a Lost Property Office what you have lost* (j'ai perdu ...), *what it was like* (il/elle est ...) *and where you lost it* (je l'ai perdu (e) ...).

Large
Brown
Plastic

Small
Black
Leather

Old
Red and green
Give the make.

New
Brown
Leather

Yellow
Plastic
Old

LOST PROPERTY, REPAIRS

EXERCISE 2

Can you sort out the following lost items and the descriptions which should go with them?

J'ai perdu . . .

mes chèques de voyage   elle est grande, noire, en plastique; tous mes vêtements sont dedans.

mon sac    il est noir, carré – et je venais d'y mettre une nouvelle pellicule.

ma montre    il y en a vingt – ils sont dans un carnet bleu.

ma valise   elle est assez grande, brune, en cuir; mes lunettes, mon porte-monnaie et mon passeport sont dedans.

mon appareil    c'est une montre à affichage numérique; c'est en acier inox.

EXERCISE 3

A game. For this you need a partner. One of you describes a piece of lost property taken from the suggestions below, and if the other person guesses correctly what it is by the time ten hints are given, s/he wins the point.

mon appareil photo
my camera

mon parapluie
my umbrella

mon bracelet
my bracelet

mon maillot de bain
my swimsuit

mon chapeau
my hat

mon imperméable
my mac

ma bague
my ring

mon auto
my car

ma caméra
my movie camera

mes gants
my gloves

What's wrong?

I've got a puncture	j'ai un pneu crevé
it isn't working	ça ne marche pas
it has broken down (of machine)	il (elle) est en panne
it's torn	il (elle) est déchiré(e)
it needs heeling	il (elle) est éculé(e)
to heel a shoe	remettre un talon à
to put a sole on a shoe	ressemeler un soulier
the sole is worn	la semelle est usée
there's a hole in my sock	il y a un trou dans ma chaussette

What do you need?

I need…	j'ai besoin de…
can you lend me	pouvez-vous me louer
bicycle pump	une pompe
fuse	un plomb, un fusible
(there's been a fuse	il y a un plomb de sauté)
needle	une aiguille
thread	un fil
repair kit	une trousse de réparation
screwdriver	un tournevis
dry cleaner's	la teinturerie
garage	un garage
shoe repairer's shop	une cordonnerie
repair shop	un atelier de réparations

EXERCISE 4

With a partner, make up some short conversations based on the following pictures. Use this dialogue to help you.

Partner 1: Excusez-moi, pouvez-vous m'aider, s'il vous plaît?
Partner 2: Qu'est-ce qu'il y a?
Partner 1 says what is wrong, and says what s/he needs.

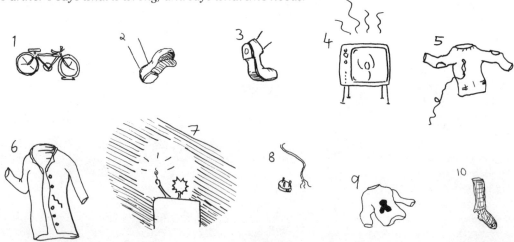

LOST PROPERTY, REPAIRS 77

EXERCISE 5 Make a set of small cards, or cut pictures out of magazines, of articles suitable for a holiday abroad which might require repair. Partner 1 chooses one at random, and decides what is wrong with the article. You have a free choice, as in the picture it will probably look perfect. Then s/he starts the dialogue described in exercise 4.

Having things repaired or cleaned

Est-ce que vous pouvez	réparer	ma montre?
Can you	*repair*	*my watch?*
C'est combien pour	nettoyer à sec	mon tricot?
How much is it to	*dry clean*	*my sweater?*
Vous allez mettre combien de temps à	laver	les vetements?
How long will you take to	*wash*	*the clothes?*

How long will it take?

Quand est-ce qu'il (elle) sera prêt(e)?
When will it be ready?
Ça va demander combien de temps?
How long will it take?
On en a pour longtemps?
Will it be long?

EXERCISE 6 Imagine you have taken the articles or vehicles mentioned in exercise 4 to a shop or garage. With a partner, make up some short conversations. Partner 1 asks (a) if the article or vehicle can be repaired, (b) how much it costs, (c) how long it will take, and (d) when it will be ready. Partner 2 gives suitable replies.

EXERCISE 7 Use cut-out pictures (those for exercise 5 will be suitable) to make up dialogues as in exercise 6.

EXERCISE 8 *Rôle playing*
1 You are complaining to the hotel manager that your watch has been stolen from your hotel bedroom. S/he asks you details of the watch – when you lost it, where exactly you left it, etc.
2 You're in a lost property office, reclaiming your lost suitcase, which you think you can see on the shelf. Unfortunately, someone who happens to be in the office also lays claim to it. Each of you has to describe in detail what is in it, according to the questions put to you by the official, e.g. does it contain any shoes/sweaters/shirts or blouses/jeans/swimwear/underwear/jewellery, etc.?
3 You have taken your shoes for repairs to the sole and heel. Explain what is required and ask for details of the cost and how long the repair will take. The owner then tries to sell you a new pair of shoes instead, which s/he says are wonderful.

CONVERSATION 1 — At the lost property office

Où se trouve le bureau des objets trouvés, s.v.p., m...?
Where's the lost property office, please?

Juste en face, m...
Just opposite.

Bonjour, m...
C'est pour quoi?
*Good afternoon.
Can I help you?*

J'ai perdu ma valise.
I've lost my suitcase.

Quand est-ce que vous l'avez perdue?
When did you lose it?

Je l'ai perdue ce matin, entre onze heures et midi.
I lost it this morning, between 11 o'clock and midday.

Où est-ce que vous l'avez perdue?
Where did you lose it?

Dans le hall d'entrée de l'hôtel Splendide
In the entrance hall of the Splendide hotel.

Qu'est-ce qu'il y avait dedans?
What was inside it?

Tous mes vêtements, quelques livres et mes chèques de voyage.
All my clothes, a few books and my traveller's cheques.

Elle est comment?
What's it like?

Elle est assez grande, en plastique noir, et mon nom est marqué dessus.
It's quite large, black plastic and my name's on it.

Bon. Revenez demain, ou téléphonez, et on vous dira si on l'a retrouvée.
Right. Come back tomorrow, or phone, and we'll tell you if it has been found.

Merci beaucoup, m...Au revoir!
Thank you very much. Goodbye!

Au revoir, m...
Goodbye!

9 Asking for information

COMMENT EST-CE QUE JE PEUX...? HOW CAN I...?

obtenir des renseignements
get some information

trouver la Mairie
find the Town Hall

trouver un agent de police
find a policeman

réserver une place
book a seat

Comment est-ce que je peux...?
How can I...?

obtenir de l'argent français
obtain some French money

garer la voiture
park the car

obtenir un 'jeton'
get a 'jeton'

acheter un billet
buy a ticket

obtenir de la monnaie
get some change

QU'EST-CE QUE JE PEUX...? WHAT CAN I...?

acheter dans ce magasin
buy in this shop

Qu'est-ce que je peux...?
What can I...?

faire pour vous aider
do to help you

voir dans les environs
see around here

faire
do

acheter pour dix francs
buy for 10 francs

VOULEZ-VOUS...? WILL YOU...?

me montrer
show me

Voulez-vous...?
Will you...?

me donner
give me

m'aider à...(+ inf.)
help me to...

me dire
tell me

m'apporter
bring me

80 ALLÔ! ALLÔ!

EXERCISE 1 *Using the information given above, can you cope with the following situations?*

1 *You need a 'jeton' in order to make a 'phone call.*
2 *You would like to buy a few souvenirs, but you have very little money left.*
3 *You want to park your car, but you have lost the keys.*
4 *You meet a little old lady wandering around the bus station, looking very lost.*
5 *You want to buy a train ticket, but the ticket office appears to be closed.*
6 *You have arrived at a small village, where your motor-bike has broken down, and you have 2 hours to wait while it is being repaired.*
7 *You would like to play a record on a juke-box, but you haven't got the correct change.*
8 *An old man has just collapsed in the street near you.*
9 *You are bored.*
10 *You want the waiter to bring you the bill.*
11 *You want your friend to help you with the washing up.*
12 *You want to know where the travel agency (**agence de voyages**) is.*
13 *You want the assistant in the Information Bureau to point out to you the position of a cathedral on a map you have.*
14 *You wish to buy two tickets for Versailles.*
15 *You want some information about the amenities provided at a youth hostel (**auberge de la jeunesse**) nearby.*

EXERCISE 2 *Imagine you have just arrived at the* syndicat d'initiative *of a town in France. Your partner is going to answer your questions. Ask for the sort of information you think you would need. Your partner must ask you a question in reply, such as:*

Do you want those that are (ceux/celles qui sont) open every day? Open on Sundays? The cheaper ones? (Les moins chers?) the dearer ones? the nearest ones? etc. and you should give a suitable reply. You can ask about hiring equipment and times of opening and closing.

Some useful vocabulary:
Will you give me some information about the . . .
Voulez-vous me donner des renseignements sur le/la/les . . .

boarding houses	les pensions (f)
camp sites	les campings (m)
castles	les châteaux (m)
excursions	les excursions (f)
exhibitions	les expositions (f)
evening amusements	les divertissements dans la soirée
festivals	les fêtes (f); (of music) festivals (m)
hotels	les hôtels (m)
information bureau	le syndicat d'initiative
monuments	les monuments historiques (m)
museums	les musées (m)
shows	les spectacles (f)
sports facilities	les équipements sportifs

Have you	*a town plan*	un plan de la ville	*please?*
	a list of hotels	une liste d'hôtels	s'il vous
Avez-vous	*some brochures*	quelques brochures	plaît?
	a map of the town	une carte de la ville	

ASKING FOR INFORMATION 81

Can one/we/you	hire bicycles	louer des vélos?
	hire skis	louer des skis?
Est-ce qu'on peut	go there every day	y aller tous les jours?

EXERCISE 3

Imagine you have been given the following brochure of events at the information bureau. Make up a dialogue with your partner about these events, asking, for example, what artists are exhibiting at the Château, where the cycle tour is going on July 2, how much the concert costs on July 4, where the cathedral and the museum are, etc. Your partner should give a suitable answer.

Useful vocabulary:
 Où se trouve... Where is...?
 Ça commence à quelle heure? When does it begin?
 Ça finit à quelle heure? When does it end?
 Ça coûte combien? How much does it cost?
 Quel est le prix de... What's the price of...?

JUILLET A AUCH

1er au 15 juillet
 Au Château de Saint-Cricq,
 "EXPOSITION DE PEINTURE"

2 juillet
 CYCLOTOURISME (Voir S.I.)

4 juillet
 18 h 30, CONCERT dans l'Heure avec un Groupe
 de musiciens gascons, dans le jardin de l'Ancien Musée (derrière la Mairie)

5 juillet
 10 h : Visite de la Cathédrale
 15 h : Visite du Musée ... guidées et gratuites

8 au 19 juillet
 A la Maison des Jeunes et de la Culture du Moulias
 "STAGE - THEATRE - Masques et Marionnettes"

9 juillet
 14 h : Présentation du Livre "HISTOIRE D'AUCH et du PAYS
 D'AUCH" à la Société Archéologique du Gers.

10 juillet
 15 h - 21 h : - Tournoi de Pétanque (non licenciés) au
 Camping Municipal
 - Circuit dans le GERS (voir S.I.)

11 au 19 juillet
 Semaine d'Animation au village de LAVARDENS

12 juillet
 10 h : Visite de la Cathédrale
 15 h : Visite du Musée

13 juillet
 20 h 30 : Promenade Nocturne avec,
 au retour, Super Grillade.
 (départ J.C. du MOULIAS)

20 août
 21 h 30 : Grande Nocturne au MUSEE (entrée libre)
 Cyclotourisme (voir S.I.)

21 août
 Circuit dans le Gers (voir S.I.)
 Tournoi de Pétanque

22 août
 14 h - 15 h : "HEURE DU CONTE" à la Bibliothèque Municipale

23 août
 RETRAITE AUX FLAMBEAUX et CONCERT

24 août
 8 h : Promenade au Bois d'Auch (S.I.)
 20 h 30 : Bal Costumé au Château de Saint-Cricq

28 août
 18 h 30 : Concert dans l'Heure avec musiciens gascons
 (Jardin Ortholan)

29 août
 Circuit dans le Gers (voir S.I.)
 14 h - 15 h : "HEURE DU CONTE" à la Bibliothèque Municipale

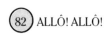 ALLÔ! ALLÔ!

Buying a ticket

Donnez-moi un/deux/trois billet(s) pour adulte/enfant pour le/la . . . s.v.p.

EXERCISE 4

Ask for one or more tickets for each of the events taking place in July at Auch. (Vary the number and type of ticket required.) Your partner will say how much you owe (Ça fait . . . s.v.p.), you will give more than is required, and s/he will give the change. E.g.

Ça fait 150 francs, s.v.p.
Voilà 200 francs.
Et voilà 50 francs que je vous rends.

EXERCISE 5

Being awkward! Each time your host suggests an outing, you welcome the suggestion, but your younger brother or sister is awkward and objects. Make up a few conversations based on the above list of events in Auch (or you can make up one of your own).

Useful phrases:
Oui, j'aimerais beaucoup faire cela.　　　　Je n'aimerais pas cela du tout.
Ce serait très intéressant.　　　　　　　　Ce serait ennuyeux.
　　　〃　　passionnant.
Ça m'intéresse beaucoup.　　　　　　　　　Ça ne m'intéresse pas.
J'aime beaucoup le scrabble　　　　　　　　Je n'aime point le scrabble
　　　　　　　les bals costumés　　　　　　　　　　　　les bals costumés
　　　　　　　la pétanque　　　　　　　　　　　　　　　la pétanque
　　　　　　　les randonnées　　　　　　　　　　　　　les randonnées

EXERCISE 6

Can you guess to what questions these are the answers?

1 Ah oui, il y a une excursion à Bordeaux tous les jours.
2 Je regrette, il n'y a plus de places pour demain.
3 Prenez la première rue à droite, et vous la verrez à gauche.
4 Il y a un car à dix heures et demie.
5 Il y a un car pour le retour à dix-huit heures exactement.
6 A la mairie.
7 Non, ce n'est pas nécessaire. Il y a toujours des places.
8 100 francs.
9 On part d'Auch, on fait le tour de tous les châteaux des environs, et enfin on dîne dans un très bon restaurant.
10 Location des voitures? Oui, c'est très facile.

CONVERSATION 1 ● At the information bureau

Où se trouve le syndicat d'initiative s.v.p.?	Where's the information bureau, please?
Just opposite.	Juste en face, m . . .
Bonjour, m . . . Pouvez-vous m'aider, s.v.p.?	*Good afternoon. Can you help me, please?*
Certainly, sir/madam. In what way?	Certainement, m . . . C'est pour quoi?

ASKING FOR INFORMATION

Avez-vous une liste d'hôtels, s.v.p.?

Have you a list of hotels, please?

Yes. There you are. And here's a plan of the town too.

Oui, m... Voilà. Et voici un plan de la ville aussi.

Je voudrais aussi des renseignements sur les excursions en car, s.v.p.

I'd also like some information about coach trips, please.

Of course. Here are a few leaflets.

Bien sûr. Voici quelques dépliants.

Où se trouve le camping le plus proche, s.v.p.?

Where's the nearest camp site, please?

Go to the end of this street, and turn right.

Allez jusqu'au bout de cette rue, et tournez à droite.

Merci beaucoup, m... Au revoir.

Thank you very much. Goodbye.

10 Minor illness, injury, road accident, doctor

QU'EST-CE QU'IL Y A?   WHAT'S THE MATTER?

au ventre
stomach

au bras
arm

à la cheville
ankle

à la jambe
leg

aux oreilles
ears

J'ai mal
I have a pain
Je me suis fait mal
I hurt

au cœur
feel sick

à la gorge
throat

au pied
foot

à la tête
head

aux yeux
eyes

aux dents
teeth

un rhume
a cold

une éruption de boutons
an outbreak of spots

une bronchite
bronchitis

une piqûre
an insect bite

J'ai
I have

une angine
sore throat

la grippe
'flu

de la fièvre
a temperature

une fracture
a fracture

MINOR ILLNESS, INJURY, ROAD ACCIDENT, DOCTOR

un médicament
some medecine

des cachets/des pilules
some pills

une lotion
a lotion

du sparadrap
some plaster

Donnez-moi
Give me
s.v.p.
please

de l'aspirine
some aspirin

une crème (antiseptique)
an (antiseptic) cream

un pansement
a bandage

EXERCISE 1

Going to the chemist's (**chez le pharmacien**). *Pretend you are at the chemist's in France. Go in turn through each of the complaints given in diagrams A and B, and ask for a suitable remedy from diagram C, e.g.*

J'ai mal au ventre. Donnez-moi un sirop, s'il vous plaît.
J'ai mal au bras. Donnez-moi une lotion, s'il vous plaît.

You can do this exercise with a partner, who pretends to be the chemist, and either tells you what the charge is, or says:

Ah, non! Il vaut mieux	aller au lit	*go to bed*
Oh no! You'd do	aller voir le docteur	*go to see the doctor*
better to	aller à l'hôpital	*go to the hospital*

EXERCISE 2

Going to the doctor's (**chez le docteur/le médecin**) *You are in the doctor's surgery. Go in turn through each of the complaints as in exercise 1. Each time, the doctor repeats what you have said, and then recommends a remedy. Instead of saying '***Donnez-moi,** of course, s/he will have to say* **Il faut prendre . . .** *or* **Il faut mettre . . .** *followed by one of the remedies in diagram C. S/he may even say*
Il faut avoir une piqûre (*an injection*).
The whole conversation should go something like this:

Doctor: Qu'est-ce qu'il y a? *or* Où est-ce que vous avez mal?
Patient: J'ai mal au ventre.
Doctor: Vous avez mal au ventre? Il faut prendre un médicament.

EXERCISE 3

A game – Crazy Doctors! Make up cards containing the drawings in diagrams A and B. Make up a number of cards giving various reasons for different ailments (**j'ai trop mangé . . . j'ai trop bu . . . Je suis tombé(e) dans la rue . . . j'ai pris un bain de soleil,** *etc.) Make a third pile of cards, each starting* **'Je vais vous donner'** *and adding pictures of the remedies in diagram C.*

 ALLÔ! ALLÔ!

Choose a partner. One of you is the doctor, one the patient. Shuffle the cards. The patient has the first two piles and the doctor has the third. Take from the top of the piles and make up dialogues to suit the pictures. The dialogues go something like this:

Patient: J'ai mal à la gorge.
Doctor: Pourquoi?
Patient: Je suis tombé(e) dans la rue.
Doctor: Je vais vous donner un pansement.

 EXERCISE 4

*Can you tell what's wrong with the following patients from the instructions given to them by the doctor? Start with either '**Il/elle a mal . . .**' or '**Il/elle a . . .**'*
1 Il faut rester au lit pendant une semaine, le pied immobilisé.
2 Il faut rester au lit pendant deux jours au moins, manger très peu, boire beaucoup d'eau et de jus de fruit, et prendre de l'aspirine trois ou quatre fois par jour.
3 Il faut vous gargariser régulièrement.
4 Vous devez aller tout de suite chez le dentiste. Vous avez perdu un plombage.
5 Je vais vous donner une ordonnance, et vous devez mettre cette lotion sur le visage deux fois par jour.
6 Il n'y a rien à faire. Il faut tout simplement prendre de l'aspirine toutes les quatre heures jusqu'à ce que vous vous sentiez mieux.
7 Vous devez aller à l'hôpital. Il faut passer la radio.
8 Je vais mettre là-dessus cette lotion et du sparadrap.
9 Vous êtes constipé(e). Je vais vous donner un bon purgatif.
10 Vous avez le corps dérangé. Je vais vous donner des pilules pour arrêter cette diarrhée.
11 Il faut vous reposer au lit; vous avez attrapé un coup de soleil.
12 Il ne faut pas porter des souliers comme ça, avec des talons trop hauts.

What happened?

Je suis tombé(e) en panne	*I had a breakdown*
J'ai eu une panne d'essence	*I ran out of petrol*
un pneu crevé	*I got a burst tyre*

Why?

J'ai oublié de vérifier *I forgot to check*	l'essence l'eau l'huile les freins les pneus les phares	*the petrol* *the water* *the oil* *the brakes* *the tyres* *the headlights*
J'ai oublié de *I forgot to*	faire le plein *fill up with petrol* regarder *look*	

MINOR ILLNESS, INJURY, ROAD ACCIDENT, DOCTOR 87

What is the result?

J'ai heurté *I bumped into*	la moto le piéton la voiture la bagnole le camion le trottoir le réverbère	*the motor-bike the pedestrian the car the car (slang) the lorry the pavement the lamp post*
La voiture *the car*	ne marche plus	*Isn't working any more*
Les freins/phares *The brakes/lights*	ne marchent plus	*aren't working any more*

EXERCISE 5 *Could you explain to a policeman what happened in the following accidents?*

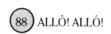 ALLÔ! ALLÔ!

 EXERCISE 6

Rôle playing.
1 *Imagine you have been taken ill while on holiday in France. Explain your symptoms to the doctor. S/he will ask you a few questions, and then give you some instructions or a prescription.*
2 *You have just had a road accident and are asking a passer-by for help. Explain what is wrong with the car, and how it happened.*
3 *You are telephoning a garage for help, as your car has broken down. Explain what is wrong, and why, and explain whereabouts you are.*

CONVERSATION 1 ● A road accident

(SCREECH OF BRAKES...)
Attention!

Look out!

Oh, I'm very sorry. Are you hurt?

Oh, je suis désolé(e). Vous êtes blessé(e)?

Oui, j'ai mal à la tête.

Yes, my head hurts.

(ANOTHER VOICE)
And I've hurt my leg.
(ANOTHER VOICE)

Et moi, je me suis fait mal à la jambe

Et moi, je me suis fait mal au dos. Au secours!

And I've hurt my back. Help!

I'll call the police. Where can I find a phone booth?

Je vais appeler la police. Où est-ce que je peux trouver une cabine téléphonique?

Par là. Juste en face.

Over there. Just opposite.

Good. I've phoned. Are you better?

Bon. J'ai téléphoné. Vous allez mieux?

Oui, mais j'ai froid.

Yes, but I'm cold.

You're cold? Here's a blanket. Are you hungry?

Vous avez froid? Voici une couverture. Vous avez faim?

Non, je n'ai pas faim, mais j'ai soif.

No, I'm not hungry, but I'm thirsty.

You're thirsty? Here's some coffee from my thermos.

Vous avez soif? Voici du café de mon thermos.

Ah, je suis fatigué(e).

Oh, I am tired.

You're tired? Wait – the ambulance is coming straightaway.

Vous êtes fatigué(e)? Attendez – l'ambulance va venir tout de suite.

MINOR ILLNESS, INJURY, ROAD ACCIDENT, DOCTOR

Est-ce qu'on va faire un constat?
Is somebody going to make a report?

Yes; and I'll give you my name and address.
Oui; et je vais vous donner mon nom et mon adresse.

CONVERSATION 2 ● Making an appointment.

Hello! Is that M. Hulot's surgery?
Allô! C'est bien le cabinet de M. Hulot?

Oui, m... Qu'est-ce qu'il y a?
Yes, m... What's the matter?

Can I have an appointment with M. Hulot, please? When is his surgery?
Est-ce que je peux prendre rendez-vous avec M. Hulot, s.v.p.? A quelle heure consulte-t-il?

Il consulte cet après-midi. Vous souffrez beaucoup?
There is a surgery this afternoon. Are you in much pain?

Yes. I have an awful toothache.
Oui, j'ai très mal aux dents.

Est-ce que vous pouvez venir dans une heure?
Can you come in an hour?

Oh yes. You are kind.
Ah oui, Vous êtes bien gentil (le).

Quel est votre nom?
What's your name?

It's ...
C'est ...

Vous êtes assuré(e)?
Are you insured?

Yes, I'm insured.
Oui, je suis assuré(e).

Bon. A tout à l'heure.
Good. See you later.

See you later!
A tout à l'heure!

11 House and home

Introducing someone

John, je te présente
John, let me introduce
OR
John, voici
John, this is

mon père
my father

ma mère
my mother

mon copain Nicholas
my friend Nicholas

ma sœur Sophie
my sister Sophie

pépé
grandad

mémé
grandma

Other useful words:
mon frère   *my brother*
mon oncle   *my uncle*
mon cousin   *my cousin*
mon prof   *my teacher*

ma copine   *my friend (female)*
ma tante   *my aunt*
ma cousine   *my cousin (female)*

EXERCISE 1

Introduce these people to your friend:

Informal
1 François(e), je te présente
2 François(e), je te présente
3 François(e), voici
4 François(e), voici
5 François(e), voici

Formal
6 M. Delain, je vous présente
7 M. Delain, je vous présente
8 Mme. Delain, je vous présente
9 Mme. Delain, je vous présente
10 Mme. Delain, je vous présente

HOUSE AND HOME

When you are introduced, you should reply in one of the following ways:
INFORMAL *(to someone of your own age):*
  'Bonjour, Jean(ne). Comment ça va?'
FORMAL *(to someone older, to whom you should show respect, such as your friend's parents):*
  'Bonjour, monsieur (madame). Comment allez-vous?'
VERY FORMAL
  'Enchanté(e), monsieur (madame).'

EXERCISE 2

Go through the introduction in exercise 1 again, this time adding a suitable reply, e.g.

1 François(e), je te présente mon copain Jules.
  Bonjour, Jules. Comment ça va?
      OR
6 M. Delain, je vous présente Madame Renoir.
  Enchanté, Madame. Je suis très heureux de faire votre connaissance.

EXERCISE 3

Divide yourselves into groups of three, and take turns to introduce one another, and give appropriate responses. You can make this more fun by making several different labels to give yourself imaginary names, and change them at random. You may choose to be, for example, your favourite pop star, a TV character, an old person, a child, a teacher, etc.
  This is not quite so easy as it sounds, because you must vary your reply according to
  (a) whether the person you address is a close friend or not (use **te** or **vous**);
  (b) whether the person you are introducing is a close friend or not. (Will you introduce them by their Christian name or their surname?)

Getting to know you

Here are some more useful questions and answers which you may need in order to get to know your new friend better.

Question	Answer
Comment t'appelles-tu? Comment vous appelez-vous? *What is your name?*	Je m'appelle François(e). *My name is François(e).*
Comment ça va? Comment allez-vous? *How are you?*	Très bien, merci. Et toi? Très bien merci. Et vous? *Very well, thank you. How are you?*
Où habites-tu? Où habitez-vous? *Where do you live?*	J'habite à . . . *I live in . . . (a town)* OR J'habite en Angleterre. *I live in England.*
Où habites-tu à présent? Où habitez-vous à présent? *Where are you living at present?*	J'habite chez Madame Lebrun. *I'm living at Madame Lebrun's.*

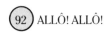 ALLÔ! ALLÔ!

Tu es arrivé(e) quand? Vous êtes arrivé(e) quand? *When did you arrive?*	Je suis arrivé(e) *I arrived* hier *yesterday* la semaine dernière *last week* il y a un mois *a month ago* lundi/mardi/mercredi/*etc.* *Monday/Tuesday/Wednesday/etc.*

Tu vas rester longtemps?
Vous allez rester longtemps?
Are you staying long?
	Encore une semaine
	   –*another week*
	Encore une quinzaine
	   –*another fortnight*
	Oui, un mois –*yes, a month*
	Non, pas longtemps – *no, not long*

Quel âge as-tu? Quel âge avez-vous? *How old are you?*	J'ai … ans *I'm* …

 EXERCISE 4

Your partner asks you the above questions, and you must answer according to the information given in the chart below. Then change roles. You could be persons 1, 3, 5, and your partner could be persons, 2, 4, 6.

Name	How are you?	Where you live	Where you are staying at present	When you arrived	Are you staying long?	Age
1 Sylvia	Well	In England	At Mrs Lebrun's	Last week	2 more weeks	16
2 Peter	Well	In London	At Mrs Leblanc's	On Monday	No	15
3 Anne	Well	In England	At Mr Rollin's	Yesterday	A month	17
4 Mark	Well	In Birmingham	At M. Lenoir's	On Tuesday	Another week	14
5 Mrs Rawlinson (use **vous**)	Well	In England	At the 'Hôtel Splendide'	Last week	2 more weeks	40
6 Mr Beckett (use **vous**)	Well	In Leicester	At the 'Hôtel Miramar'	On Saturday	No	42

 EXERCISE 5

Make up seven piles of cards. Each pile gives information according to the columns above. E.g. one pile contains names, another pile contains ages, and so on. Turn up the top card on each pile, and answer your partner's questions according to the information you have turned up. Then change rôles. Remember that if you are taking the part of an older person, your partner must address you as **vous**.

HOUSE AND HOME (93)

EXERCISE 6

Rôle-playing.
1 *You are at a disco in France with your pen-friend, who introduces you to his French friend. Make up an imaginary conversation, asking your new friend questions as well as giving replies.*
2 *You are at a French school with your French pen-friend, who introduces you to his/her headmaster. Imagine the ensuing conversation.*
3 *Choose a partner. One of you is a new French friend arriving to stay at an English home; the other is the young person welcoming him/her. The 'French friend' thinks of 10 questions s/he might ask on arrival, e.g. about:*

> *The times of meals and bedtime;*
> *the amenities of your house such as toilet, bathroom and bedroom;*
> *the places and kinds of entertainment;*
> *the places of interest to visit.*
>
> *The partner gives possible answers.*

"M. le Directeur, je vous présente mon correspondant français."

CONVERSATION 1   Arriving at your pen-friend's house

Ah, bonjour! Entrez! Voulez-vous vous asseoir?	*Ah, hello! Come in! Would you like to sit down?*
Thank you very much. How are you?	Merci beaucoup,. Comment allez-vous?
Très bien, merci. Vous n'êtes pas trop fatigué(e)?	*Very well, thank you. You're not too tired?*
Oh no . . . I've brought you a little present from England.	Ah non . . . Je vous ai apporté un petit cadeau d'Angleterre.

Ah, vous êtes bien gentil(le)! Merci beaucoup. Venez; je vais vous montrer votre chambre.

Oh, you are kind! Thank you very much. Come; I'll show you your room.

Where's the bathroom, please?

Où se trouve la salle de bains, s'il vous plaît?

La voici.

Here it is.

May I have a shower, please?

Est-ce que je peux prendre une douche, s.v.p.?

Mais bien sûr. Avez-vous tout ce qu'il vous faut?

Of course. Have you everything you need?

I need some soap, a towel and some toothpaste, please.

J'ai besoin de savon, d'une serviette et de dentifrice, s.v.p.

Voilà.

There you are.

Thank you very much. You are very kind.

Merci beaucoup. Vous êtes très gentil(le).

De rien! Ça me fait plaisir.

Not at all! It's a pleasure.

CONVERSATION 2 ● Discussing daily routine

Bon, on va causer un peu. A quelle heure vous couchez-vous généralement?

Right, let's have a little chat. What time do you go to bed usually?

About ten o'clock.

A dix heures à peu près.

Et vous vous levez quand?

And when do you get up?

That depends. I get up between eight and nine o'clock during the holidays.

Ça dépend. Je me lève entre huit et neuf heures pendant les vacances.

Quelles sont les heures des repas chez vous?

What are your mealtimes at home?

*I have breakfast at eight o'clock.
I have lunch at twelve.
I have the evening meal at six.*

Je prends le petit déjeuner à huit heures.
Je déjeune à midi.
Je dîne à six heures.

Pas de goûter?

Don't you have tea?

Oh yes, we have tea at 4.

Ah si, on goûte à quatre heures.

HOUSE AND HOME

Et maintenant, vous avez des questions à me poser?

Well now, have you any questions?

Can I help you with the housework?

Est-ce que je peux vous aider à faire le ménage?

Ah, ça, c'est gentil! Qu'est-ce que vous savez faire?

Oh, that's nice of you! What can you do?

At home I set the table, I clear the table and I wash up.

Chez moi je mets la table, je débarrasse la table et je fais la vaisselle.

Eh bien, si vous m'aidez à faire la vaisselle, ça sera très gentil.

Well then, if you help me to wash up, that will be very nice of you.

I'll be very willing to.

Volontiers.

CONVERSATION 3 • Introducing someone

(MARIE) Bonjour, Jean

(MARIE) Hello, John

*Hello Marie.
  How's things?*

Bonjour, Marie.
  Comment ça va?

Très bien, merci. Et toi?

Fine, thanks. What about you?

Fine, thanks.

Très bien, merci.

Jean, voici Mark, mon correspondant anglais.

Jean, this is Mark, my English pen-friend.

Ah, hello, Mark. When did you get here?

Ah, bonjour, Mark. Tu es arrivé quand?

(MARK) Hier seulement.

(MARK) Just yesterday.

You must feel a bit strange then. Are you staying long?

Tu dois te sentir un peu dépaysé alors. Tu vas rester longtemps?

Une quinzaine.

A fortnight.

Oh, after a fornight you'll be able to manage. Where do you live in England?

Ah, au bout d'une quinzaine tu sauras te débrouiller. Où est-ce que tu habites en Angleterre?

 ALLÔ! ALLÔ!

J'habite à Londres.	*I live in London.*
Oh, I know London. I spent a week there last year.	Ah, je connais Londres. J'y ai passé une semaine l'année dernière.
Ça t'a plu?	*Did you like it?*
Yes, it was very interesting. I say, Marie, I could phone you up, and we could get together again. What's your phone number?	Oui, c'était très intéressant. Dis donc, Marie, je pourrais te donner un coup de téléphone, et on pourrait se revoir. Quel est ton numéro de téléphone?
Vingt-deux zéro quatre.	*2204*
O.K. See you later!	Bon. A tout à l'heure!
A tout à l'heure!	*See you!*

12. Places of entertainment

entrer — *go in*
réserver une place — *book a seat*
(Quand) est-ce que je peux . . .? — *(When) can I . . .?*
fumer — *smoke*
donner un pourboire à l'ouvreuse — *give a tip to the usherette*
voir le directeur — *see the manager*
acheter un billet (ticket) pour la matinée — *buy a ticket for the matinée performance*

How much does it cost?

C'est combien, une place *How much does a seat cost*	au balcon *in the balcony?* à l'orchestre *in the stalls?* près/loin de l'écran *near/a long way from the screen?* près/loin de la scène *near/a long way from the stage?* pour adulte *for an adult?* pour enfant *for a child?*

What's on

Qu'est-ce qu'on joue au théâtre?   *What's on at the theatre?*
Qu'est-ce qui passe au cinéma?   *What's on at the cinema?*

Any reductions?

Est-ce qu'il y a *Is there*	un tarif spécial *a special price*	pour les enfants? *for children?*
	un tarif réduit *a reduced rate*	pour les étudiants? *for students?*
	un rabais *a reduction*	pour les groupes? *for a group?*

ALLÔ! ALLÔ!

un western
a western

doublé
dubbed

une tragédie
a tragedy

Est-ce que c'est...?
Is it...?

en anglais
in English

un film américain
an American film

un documentaire
a documentary

une comédie
a comedy

avec des sous-titres
with sub-titles

en couleur
in colour

en noir et blanc
black and white

un film de gangsters
a gangster film

When does it begin?

A quelle heure commence/finit What time	la première séance	does the first performance begin/end?
	la dernière séance	does the last performance begin/end?
	la matinée	does the matinee begin/end?
	l'entracte	does the interval begin/end?
	la mi-temps	does the half-time begin/end?

Choosing a show

Quand est-ce que ça commence When does it begin,	la séance	the performance?
	le concert	the concert?
	le cirque	the circus?
	le match	the match?
	le festival	the (musical) festival?
	le son-et-lumière	the son-et-lumière?

EXERCISE Look at the advertisements for shows and matches and, with a partner, see how many questions you can ask and answer about when there is a show or match, how much it costs, when it begins and ends. Use the vocabulary given above to help you, and invent the prices if they aren't given. Then buy some tickets, saying where you want to sit (if relevant). The assistant will give you a price, and if you offer more, will say what the change is.

22, rue Jacob   326.36.26

ROTISSERIE DE L'ABBAYE

SAINT-GERMAIN-DES-PRÉS

Dans un cadre exceptionnel sous les voûtes du XIII ᵉ siècle, une ambiance du tonnerre de 20 h à 2 h.
DINER-SPECTACLE-CABARET de qualité, d'humour, de fantaisie. Dîners de groupe · PARKING

PLACES OF ENTERTAINMENT

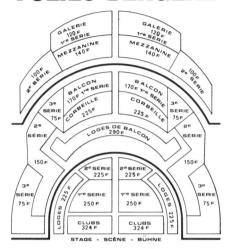

FOLIES BERGERE

PRIX VALABLES JUSQU'AU 31 DÉCEMBRE 1985

2 spectacles tous les soirs à 20 h.15 et 22 h. 10
RELACHE LUNDI
Informations et Réservations
Tous les jours de 11 h à 18 h 30 au Théâtre ou par téléphone 246.77.11
Par correspondance : 8, rue Saulnier, 75009 Paris, Telex 641 533 F
Et auprès des Agences et Concierges d'Hôtels

PROGRAMME DU MOIS DE MAI

Date	Jour/Heure	Type	Titre	Pages
2	MERCREDI 15 H	CINE-CLUB ENFANTS	la petite fille, le chien et le phoque	17
4	VENDREDI 21 H	CONCERT	audition du conservatoire	19
5	SAMEDI 21 H	THEATRE	compagnons d'arlequin	22
8	MARDI 17 H 15 / 20 H 45	CONNAIS. DU MONDE	la mer rouge	23
10	JEUDI 21 H	CONCERT	concert musique municipale	19
11	VENDREDI 21 H	VARIETES	LES COMPAGNONS DE LA CHANSON	24
15	MARDI 21 H	CINE-CLUB	2001, l'odyssée de l'espace	17
17 18	JEUDI VENDREDI	SPECTACLE ENFANTS	théâtre à vendre	20
18 au 25	VENDREDI VENDREDI	EXPOSITION	france - r.d.a.	21
17	JEUDI 21 H	CONCERT	arts et musique en soissonnais	21
22	MARDI 21 H	THEATRE	mooney et ses caravanes et rupture	23
23	MERCREDI 15 H	CINE-CLUB ENFANTS	la potion qui fait grandir les petits et rapetisser les grands	17
29	MARDI 21 H.	CONNAIS. DU MONDE	l'everest	23
31	JEUDI 21 H	CONCERT	orchestre départemental	22

Le Broadway — BAR ouvert 17 h à 2 h mat
En soirée le pianiste Sud Américain
ARMANDO CARDOSO
1, rue d'Armaillé, angle av. Carnot
380.05.69 — F. dimanche

CLUB ZED — 2, RUE DES ANGLAIS (5ᵉ)
M° Maubert - 033.93.78
Tous les jours de 22 h à l'aube
FERMÉ LUNDI (Park. Lagrange)
DISCOTHÈQUE DANSANTE

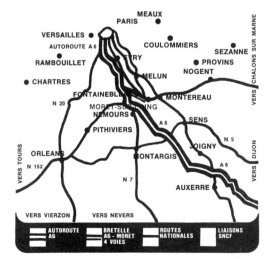

MORET-SUR-LOING
PRÈS DE FONTAINEBLEAU
SAISON 1985 - 18ᵉ ANNÉE

SÉANCES TOUS LES SAMEDIS
DU 22 JUIN AU 7 SEPTEMBRE

22-29 JUIN - 6-13-20-27 JUILLET, A 22 H 30
3-10-17-24-31 AOUT - VENDREDI 16 AOUT et 7 SEPTEMBRE,
A 22 HEURES
Séances à la nuit tombée...

Places réservées (chaises numérotées)   50 F (1), enfants 40 F (jusqu'à 12 ans)
Places non réservées   35 F (2), enfants 25 F (jusqu'à 12 ans)
Billets de groupe minimum 20 personnes (uniquement sur réservation)

(1) Les places numérotées ne seront plus assurées 10 minutes avant le début du spectacle. Ouverture des guichets : 1 heure avant le début des séances.
(2) Places assises dans la limite des disponibilités.

Les règlements se font sur place, à la remise des billets.

RÉSERVATION
Par correspondance : Festival de Moret - Office de Tourisme, S.I.
77250 Moret-sur-Loing
Par téléphone   (6) 070.41.66
Sur place   à l'Office de Tourisme
                   place de Samois (sauf le lundi)

Photographie : Gilbert Petit - Impression : Imprimerie du Paroi - Typographie : SM & Co

RENSEIGNEMENTS PRATIQUES
DATES DES SPECTACLES 1985

- **JUIN à 22 h** : Vendredi 28, Samedi 29.
- **JUILLET à 22 h** : Vendredi 5, Samedi 6, Vendredi 12, Samedi 13.
- **AOUT à 21 h 30** : Samedi 10, Dimanche 11, Mercredi 14, Samedi 17, Dimanche 18, Samedi 24, Dimanche 25, Samedi 31.

HORAIRES : Ouverture du Parc à 21 heures en Juin et Juillet - 20 h 30 en Août.

Durée du spectacle : 2 heures 30.

PRIX DES PLACES :	Non Réservées	Réservées
Adultes	40,00	45,00
Groupe et carte vermeille	35,00	40,00
Enfants 5 à 12 ans	20,00	23,00
Groupe enfants	18,00	20,00

INFORMATIONS ET RÉSERVATIONS :

Courrier : Spectacle au château de Valençay, B.P. 23, 36600 VALENÇAY.
Règlement par chèque à l'ordre de CAPVAL.
Téléphone : Du 15 juin au 31 Août : Bureau de Tourisme — (54) 00.04.42.
En dehors de ces périodes : Mairie de Valençay — (54) 00.14.33.

" LE SAINT " club disco-pop
7 rue St Séverin (5ᵉ) 325.50.04 - Mᵒ St Michel. F. Lundi
CAVE PSYCHEDELIQUE - DISC.-JOCKEY PROFESSIONNEL
DISCO de 22 h à 3 h. Ensuite : musique d'écoute (pop, Jazz, etc.)
Petit déjeuner - Petit snack - Tenue originale appréciée

DISCOTHEQUE WHISKY A GOGO
Hallucinant et Fantastique
son lasershow
TOUS LES SOIRS de 21 h 30 à l'AUBE
PRIX entrée et consommation t.t.c. 30 F
(Vendredi et Samedi 35 F)
Matinée dimanche et fêtes 15 h 25 F
57, rue de Seine. 325.64.87/633.74.99

CRISS bar
MARIE-THE et ses hôtesses
vous accueillent chaque jour
de 18 h à l'aube
214, rue St Maur (10ᵉ) - 209.57.41

WONDER CLUB, 38 rue du Dragon (6ᵉ). St-Germain-des-Prés. 548.90.52. Danse Tls de 21h à l'aube. Sam., Dim et Fêtes Mat à 15h. Ent. et consom. : 20 F s.c. (Ven, Sam : 25 F).

ZED CLUB, 2, rue des Anglais (5ᵉ) (angle rue Galande). 033.93.78. Tls à partir de 22h (sf Lun). Disco. dansante.

VERSAILLES
Sur les bords du bassin de Neptune
un divertissement inoubliable
LE TRIOMPHE DE NEPTUNE
accompagné de
FEU D'ARTIFICE ET GRANDES EAUX LUMINEUSES
Samedis: 20, 27 juillet
à 22 h 15
3, 10, 17, 24 août, 7 septembre à 22 h
jeudi 16 août à 22 h

Réservations	
A Versailles	A Paris
Office de Tourisme	Agence E.R. Perrossier
7, rue des Réservoirs	Tél. 260.58.31
Tél. 950.36.22	Agence Champs-Elysées Daisy
	Tél. 359.24.60

PLACES OF ENTERTAINMENT 101

STÉRÉO-CLUB
Soirée 22 h à l'aube - Consom. 35 F
SIMONE et ses charmantes hôtesses
6, r. Arsène-Houssaye - 561-07-32 - F. dim.

STADIUM TOTEM, 66, av. d'Ivry (13ᵉ). 583.11.00. Cons. de 4 à 15 F. 12, 13-14 avril : James Newton/Antony Davis, duo.

TRAFALGAR, 54, rue Pigalle (9ᵉ). 874.66.00 et 526.05.35. Ouvert Tls de 18h à l'aube : Christian Joudinaud au piano. On peut danser.

DISCOTHEQUES

ARLEQUIN, 3, rue du Four. 326.60.70. A partir de 22h30. Tls Discotheque, promotion nouveaux « tubes ».

BARBARY COAST SALOON, 11, rue Jules-Chaplain (6ᵉ). 033.68.87. Tls de 21h à l'aube. Danse. Matinée dimanche.

BISTROTHEQUE, 3, rue de Castiglione (1ᵉʳ). 260.37.80. Discothèque 22h à l'aube. Consom. env. 40 F.

LA CASITA-CLUB, 167, rue Montmartre. Cen. 57.50. Ouv. tt. la nuit. Mat. Dim.

EXERCISE 2

Can you complete the following sentences, using the information on page 102?
1 Mémé ne voit pas bien; elle veut donc une place . . .
2 Ça coûte combien, une place . . . ?
3 L'ouvreuse a été très impolie car je ne lui ai pas donné de . . . ;
4 Je veux me plaindre du film; quand est-ce que . . .
5 Je n'ai pas vu très clairement les visages des acteurs car j'étais . . .
6 Est-ce que c'est . . . ? Je préfère les pièces comiques.
7 Mon mari préfère toujours les . . . mais moi, j'aime les documentaires.
8 Je suis arrivé trop tôt, je le sais, mais je ne veux pas rester dehors car il pleut; quand . . . ?
9 Je veux me plaindre; il y a des enfants . . . qui jettent des peaux d'orange.
10 C'est un vieux film; est-ce que c'est . . . ou . . . ?

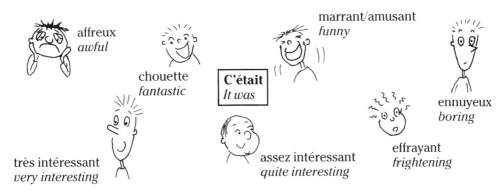

affreux / *awful*
chouette / *fantastic*
marrant/amusant / *funny*
C'était / *It was*
ennuyeux / *boring*
très intéressant / *very interesting*
assez intéressant / *quite interesting*
effrayant / *frightening*

What did you think of it?

EXERCISE 3

Revision. Can you deal with the following situations? **1** Ask the way to the nearest cinema. **2** Ask when the first performance begins. **3** Ask if you can book two seats for the stalls for tomorrow. **4** Ask how much it will cost. **5** Ask your friend if s/he'd like to go to the theatre with you. **6** Ask where you can reserve seats. **7** Ask if the film's a comedy. **8** Ask your friend if s/he'd like to sit in the stalls or in the balcony. **9** Remind your friend that it's necessary to give a tip to the usherette. **10** Ask when you're allowed to go in. **11** Ask some one what s/he thought of the film. **12** Say that it was very interesting. **13** Say that it was amusing. **14** Say that it was awful. **15** Ask when the last performance ends.

102 ALLÔ! ALLÔ!

● "Quatre places au balcon, s'il vous plaît".

EXERCISE 4

Rôle playing.

1 *Imagine that you're phoning a friend to invite him/her to the cinema or theatre with you. Discuss the various films or plays that are on, and the prices, decide on one and arrange to meet.*
2 *Imagine that you are trying to find a certain cinema in a strange French town. Ask a passer-by the way, then book two seats, and ask when the performance begins and ends. Discuss with your friend a previous film you saw featuring the same film star.*
3 *Imagine that you are at a French cinema, but you are not having a very successful time. First you don't have the correct change for the tickets, then you go into the cinema while smoking, and are told that this is not allowed. The usherette takes you to the wrong seats, and finally you forget to give her a tip.*

CONVERSATION 1 ● Going to the cinema

Deux orchestres, s.v.p., pour 'La Belle et la Bête'.	Two seats in the stalls, please, for 'Beauty and the Beast'.
Near the screen?	Près de l'écran?
Oui, s.v.p.	*Yes, please.*
That's 50f. 40, please	Ça fait cinquante francs quarante, s.v.p.
Je regrette, je n'ai pas de monnaie.	*I'm sorry, I haven't any change.*
It doesn't matter. Thank you, m . . .	Ça ne fait rien. Merci, m . . .

La séance a commencé?

No, not yet.

Eh bien, allons acheter un programme et boire quelque chose . . . Quelle sorte de films préfères-tu?

I prefer comedies.

Moi, je préfère les westerns et les films de gangsters.

Is the film tonight in colour?

Non, il est en noir et blanc, car c'est un vieux film français.

Is it dubbed?

Non, mais il y a des sous-titres.

Has the performance begun?

Non, pas encore.

Well, let's go and buy a programme and have a drink . . . What sort of films do you prefer?

Je préfère les comédies.

I prefer cowboy films and gangsters.

Le film ce soir, il est en couleur?

No, it's in black and white, because it's an old French film.

Il est doublé?

No, but there are sub-titles.

13 At a garage or petrol station

 super *4-star*

 ordinaire *2-star*

 libre-service *self-service*

 un(e) pompiste *pump attendant*

 l'essence(f) *petrol*

 l'huile(f) *oil*

 la plaque de police *registration plate*

 en panne *broken down*

 la marque *make*

 la clé *key*

 la carte routière *road map*

 les pièces(f) de rechange *spare parts*

 un essuie-glace *windscreen wiper*

 le rétroviseur *rear-view mirror*

 les phares(m) *headlights*

 le coffre *boot*

 le pare-brise *windscreen*

 la portière *door*

 le toit *roof*

 le siège *seat*

 le volant *steering wheel*

 la roue de secours *spare wheel*

 le clignotant *indicator*

 le pneu *tyre*

le numéro minéralogique/ d'immatric- ulation *registration number*

AT A GARAGE OR PETROL STATION

EXERCISE 1

Draw or trace the pictures opposite (without their names) on to 25 separate pieces of card or paper, with a partner. Place them in a pile, upside down. The first player turns up the top card, and if s/he can give the name of the picture, s/he wins the card. If not, the opponent wins the card. The winner is the one with most cards at the end.

This game is more interesting if you also put a in a few cards with instructions such as 'Miss a turn', 'Give 1/2/3 cards to your opponent', etc.

Buying petrol and checking the car.

Voulez-vous *Will you*	me donner *give me*	vingt litres de super, s.v.p. *20 litres of 4-star petrol, please.* trente litres d'ordinaire, s.v.p. *30 litres of 2-star petrol, please.*
Pouvez-vous *Can you*	vérifier *check* réparer *repair*	l'huile *the oil* l'eau *the water* les pneus *the tyres* le moteur *the engine* les freins *the brakes* l'embrayage *the clutch* le feu arrière *the rear light* les feux de position *sidelights* l'accélérateur *the accelerator*
Faites le plein, s'il vous plaît		*Fill the tank, please.*
Est-ce que c'est la bonne route pour Nice? *Is it the right road for Nice?* Pour aller à Nice, c'est quelle route, s'il vous plaît? *To get to Nice, it's which road, please?*		

EXERCISE 2

Choose a partner. One of you is the customer and one the petrol attendant. Ask the attendant the following ten questions; s/he must give a sensible reply from the answers provided.

1 *Ask for 10 litres of 2-star petrol.*
2 *Ask how much 25 litres of 4-star petrol costs.*
3 *Ask for a road map.*
4 *Ask for the tyres to be checked.*
5 *Ask for the brakes to be repaired.*
6 *Ask if the garage has any spare parts for a Ford.*
7 *Ask the attendant to fill up with petrol.*
8 *Ask for a check on the oil and water levels.*
9 *Ask if a tyre can be repaired immediately.*
10 *Ask the attendant to put the spare tyre into the boot.*

Choose from: Ah, non ne peut pas faire cela tout de suite, m . . .   Pour cela, il faut aller à la caisse . . .   Ah, non, m . . ., nous n'en avons pas pour cette marque . . .   Certainement, tout de suite, m . . .   Cent vingt francs, m . . .   Oui, je veux bien – vous avez la clef, s'il vous plaît?

 ALLÔ! ALLÔ!

 EXERCISE 3

Rôle playing.
1 *Ask for directions to the nearest garage. When you arrive, describe what's wrong with your motor-bike, and arrange to have it repaired.*
2 *You're at a petrol station. Buy some petrol and oil, ask the attendant to clean the windscreen, ask where the toilets are, and whether you can buy some food.*

● "Vous n'avez pas très bien nettoyé mon pare-brise!"

 EXERCISE 4

You are thinking of hiring a car in France. Your partner is the agent for the cars you see on the illustration.
Ask questions about each car (which you must name), such as:

    What size is it?
    How many doors/seats has it?
    Is it air-conditioned?
    Does it have a large boot?
    Has it a radio?
    How much does it cost to hire per day/per kilometre?

See if you can think of other questions. Your partner gives answers from the information provided.

AT A GARAGE OR PETROL STATION (107)

LES TARIFS DU 1er LOUEUR EN FRANCE
Train + auto
SNCF

AVIS : AGENT PRINCIPAL

Catégorie		Marque et modèle		Portes	Places	Par jour		Par km
		BOITE MECANIQUE						
Petite	A	Opel Corsa Ford Fiesta ou similaire	♪	2	4	H.T. T.T.C.	148,00 197,33	1,91 2,55
	B	Peugeot 205 Renault 5 Fiat Uno 60 ou similaire	♪	4	4	H.T. T.T.C.	161,60 215,47	2,18 2,91
Moyenne	C	Peugeot 309 Ford Escort Opel Kadett ou similaire	♪	4	4/5	H.T. T.T.C.	185,40 247,20	2,62 3,49
Routière	E	Volvo 360 BMW 316 Renault 21 Ford Sierra ou similaire	🧳 ♪	4	4/5	H.T. T.T.C.	245,50 327,33	3,13 4,17
	F	Renault 25 GTS Ford Scorpio 2L GLI (ABS) Peugeot 505 SR ou similaire	🧳 ♪	4	4/5	H.T. T.T.C.	289,00 385,33	3,31 4,41
	H	Mercedes 190 E BMW 320 i ou similaire	🧳 ♪	4	4	H.T. T.T.C.	332,00 442,67	3,78 5,04
		BOITE AUTOMATIQUE						
Ville	D	Opel Kadett automatique Volvo 340 automatique Ford Orion 1600 automatique Ford Escort 1600 automatique ou similaire	♪	4	4	H.T. T.T.C.	223,75 298,33	2,39 3,19
Luxe	M	Mercedes 230 E automatique (ABS)	✻ 🧳 ♪	4	5	H.T. T.T.C.	445,00 593,33	4,70 6,27
	I	Mercedes 280 SE automatique* (ABS) Mercedes 300 SE automatique* (ABS)	✻ 🧳 ♪	4	5	H.T. T.T.C.	636,00 848,00	7,14 9,52
		VEHICULES SPECIAUX						
Familiale	K	Peugeot 505 familiale	♪	4	7	H.T. T.T.C.	266,00 354,67	3,70 4,93
Convertible	L	Peugeot 205 cabriolet** Peugeot 205 GTI***	♪	2	4	H.T. T.T.C.	337,35 449,80	3,35 4,47
Minibus	N	Ford Transit Combi**** C 25 Combi****	♪	3	8	H.T. T.T.C.	302,00 402,67	2,70 3,60

Prix valables au 1/06/86

Disponible : * Paris - Côte d'Azur - Strasbourg
     ** Nice - Cannes - Antibes
     *** Paris - Côte d'Azur
     **** Certaines agences Avis seulement.
Durée minimum de location : 1 jour (24 heures).
Heures supplémentaires : 1/3 du prix journalier.

ABS : Système de freinage anti-blocage
🧳 Grand coffre - ♪ Radio - ✻ Air conditionné
H.T., Hors Taxe - T.T.C., Toutes Taxes Comprises à 33,33 %

CONVERSATION 1 ● At the petrol station

Où se trouve la station-service la plus proche, s.v.p.?

Where's the nearest petrol station, please?

Go straight on; it's 100 metres away.

Continuez tout droit; c'est à cent metres.

Faites le plein, s.v.p.

Fill the tank, please.

Do you want 4-star or 2-star?

Super ou ordinaire?

ALLÔ! ALLÔ!

C'est combien le litre?	*How much are they?*
4-star's 3.5 francs a litre; 2-star's 3.3 francs a litre	Le super est à trois francs cinq le litre; l'ordinaire est à trois francs trois.
Je vais prendre du super. Voulez-vous vérifier l'huile aussi?	*I'll have the 4-star. Will you check the oil too?*
Yes, sir – it's O.K. Is that all?	Oui, monsieur – ça va. C'est tout?
Non. Avez-vous une carte routière, s.v.p.? – Je vous dois combien?	*No. Have you a road map, please? – How much do I owe you?*
70 francs please.	Soixante-dix francs, s.v.p.
Voici cent francs.	*Here's 100 francs.*
And there's 30 francs change. Thank you, sir.	Et voilà trente francs que je vous rends. Merci, monsieur.
L'autoroute est à quelle distance?	*How far is it to the motorway?*
Oh, it's a long way.	Ah, c'est loin.
La ville la plus proche est à quelle distance?	*How far is the nearest town?*
20 kilometres.	A vingt kilomètres.
Et l'hôtel le plus proche?	*And the nearest hotel?*
Very near – 2 kilometres	Tout près – à deux kilomètres
Est-ce qu'on peut acheter des bonbons et des boissons ici?	*Can we buy sweets and drinks here?*
Yes – at the cash desk	Oui – à la caisse.
Est-ce qu'on peut se servir des toilettes, s.v.p.?	*May we use the toilets, please?*
Certainly, sir. Over there.	Certainement, monsieur. Là-bas.
Merci beaucoup.	*Thank you very much.*
Thank you; good-bye.	Merci, et au revoir.

Summary of useful phrases

agreeing
  I agree Je suis d'accord
  I don't agree Je ne suis pas d'accord
  Do you agree? Tu es (vous êtes) d'accord?
allowed
  It isn't allowed Ce n'est pas permis
apologising
  I'm sorry Pardon/Je m'excuse
  I'm very sorry Je suis désolé(e)
appreciation
  Thank you very much indeed! Merci mille fois!
careful
  Be careful! Attention!
certain
  I'm certain of it J'en suis sûr(e)/certain(e)
  I'm not certain of it Je n'en suis pas sûr(e)/certain(e)
  Are you sure? Tu es sûr(e)?
  it's certain/not certain C'est certain/ce n'est pas certain
  Is is certain? C'est certain?/Est-ce certain?
compliment
  It suits you Ça vous va bien
  It's delightful C'est ravissant!
  You're very kind Tu es (vous êtes) bien gentil(le)
congratulating
  congratulations! félicitations!
disappointment
  I'm (very) disappointed Je suis (très) déçu(e)
doing
  Will you do . . . Veux-tu (voulez-vous) faire . . .
  Will you go . . . Veux-tu (voulez-vous) aller . . .
doubt
  I doubt it (very much) J'en doute (fort)/Je n'en suis pas sûr(e)
  I doubt whether s/he'll come Je doute qu'il/elle vienne
  without doubt sans aucun doute
fear
  I'm afraid J'ai peur
  Are you afraid Tu as (vous avez) peur?
  I fear that . . . Je crains que . . .
having to
  I have to Je dois/il faut
  I mustn't Je ne dois pas/il ne faut pas
  I/you don't have to Ce n'est pas nécessaire/obligatoire
helping
  Help! Au secours!
  Can I help you? Je peux t'(vous) aider?
  No thank you, I'm all right Non, merci – tout va bien
  Will you help me? Veux-tu (voulez-vous) m'aider?
hope
  I hope that J'espère que
intend
  I intend to . . . Je compte . . .
  What do you intend to do? Qu'est-ce que tu comptes faire?
  Qu'est-ce vous comptez faire?
interested
  I'm interested in . . . Je m'intéresse à . . .
  Are you interested in . . . ? Ça t'intéresse, le . . . ?
  Ça vous intéresse, le . . . ?
know
  do you know him/her? Tu le(la) connais?
  Vous le (la) connaissez?
pleased/satisfied
  I'm pleased/satisfied Je suis content(e)
  I'm very pleased with it Ça me plaît beaucoup
  it's charming/delightful/delicious/super C'est charmant/ravissant/délicieux/formid/sensass
  I'm not (very) pleased with it Ça ne me plaît pas (beaucoup)
  I'm not al all pleased with it Ça ne me plaît pas du tout
possible
  Do you think it's possible? Tu crois que c'est possible?
  I think it's possible Je pense que c'est possible
  It's impossible C'est impossible/Ce n'est pas possible
  Is it possible? C'est possible? Est-ce possible?
  Is it impossible? C'est impossible? Ce n'est pas possible?
prefer
  I prefer Je préfère
  What do you prefer? Qu'est-ce que tu préfères/vous préférez?
probable
  It's probable/not probable C'est probable/Ce n'est pas probable
  Is it probable? C'est probable? Est-ce probable?
problem
  There's no problem! Pas de problème!
regret
  I regret Je regrette
remember
  I remember . . . Je me rappelle . . .
  Do you remember . . . Tu te rappelles/Vous vous rappelez?
sorry
  See 'apologising' and 'sympathy'
surprise
  I'm surprised! Tiens! /Ça m'étonne!
sympathy
  I'm very sorry Je suis désolé(e)
true
  It's true c'est vrai
  It's not true Ce n'est pas vrai
want
  I want Je veux
  Do you want . . . ? Tu veux . . . ? Vous voulez . . . ?
  What do you want? Qu'est-ce que tu veux?
  Qu'est-ce que vous voulez?

Suggested aural questions for use with the cassette

LESSON 1
Arriving at a camp site, youth hostel or hotel

Conversation 1 At a camp site
1. What is the holidaymaker's first question?
2. How long is s/he intending to stay?
3. Where would s/he settle the bill?
4. What three questions does s/he ask about the amenities?
5. Why does s/he decide not to stay after all? Where is s/he going instead?

Conversation 2 At a hotel
1. How many are there in the party, and how long are they staying?
2. On what floor are the rooms, and what additional facility do they have?
3. What is the cost per person per night? What is included in the price?
4. What does the hotelkeeper ask for?
5. What does the traveller want to do immediately?

LESSON 2
Asking the way

Conversation 1 Asking the way
1. How do you get to (a) the town hall (b) the station? (c) the Métro?
2. How do you get to the information bureau?
3. How far away is the nearest bus stop?
4. What building is 100 metres away?
5. What offer is made by the person answering the questions?

Conversation 2 I can't understand!
1. What means of transport does the Frenchwoman first suggest?
2. What directions does the Frenchwoman give for finding the bus stop?
3. What does the enquirer ask the Frenchwoman to do to make herself more easily understood?
4. What directions are given for finding the Métro?
5. What is the final means of transport suggested?

LESSON 3
Shopping

Conversation 1 At the department store
1. What part of the store is the shopper looking for?
2. Which floor is it on?
3. What is near the cash desk?
4. Where is the staircase?

Conversation 2 Buying a present
1. What article, of what size, is the shopper looking for?
2. What three materials is the shopper given to choose from?
3. What are the prices of the two articles offered by the assistant?
4. What special service does the assistant offer?
5. What are the opening and closing times of the shop?

Conversation 3 Shopping for food
1–8 What eight articles of food does the man buy?
9. What is the value of the note given by the man?
10. In the discussion following, how much does the man say he owes?
11. How much change does he say he should receive?
12. How much change has he been given?

LESSON 4
Travel by train, coach or plane

Conversation 1 Booking a ticket
1. What kind of ticket, and what class, does the traveller want?
2. What is the cost?
3. What time does the train leave? What kind of a train is it?
4. How long does the journey take, and what platform does it leave from?
5. Why can't the traveller sit where s/he would like to?

Conversation 2 Travel by bus
1. What type of vehicle is going to Nantes the next day, and at what time?
2. How many tickets does the traveller buy? Single or return?
3. What is the time of arrival at Nantes?
4. Where do people get on and off?
5. How often do the buses run to the bus station?

SUGGESTED AURAL QUESTIONS

Conversation 3   Informing some one of your arrival
1. What is Martin's first question?
2. Why is Martin phoning?
3. What day, and at what time, does Martin hope to arrive at Soissons?
4. What promise does Martin's friend make?

LESSON 5
Arranging to meet somone

Conversation 1   Arranging to meet someone
1. What invitation does Paul give to Marie?
2. Where and when does he want to meet her?
3. What time does she suggest instead?
4. Why is Paul upset later on?
5. What excuse does Marie give?

LESSON 6
At a post office or bank; at the customs desk

Conversation 1   At the post office
1. What does the customer wish to send, and where?
2. What will be the final cost of the stamps?
3. What other two articles does the customer ask for?

Conversation 2   In the phone booth
1. When Paul asks for Madam Lenoir, what question is he asked in return?
2. What instruction is then given to Paul?
3. Why can't Paul speak to Madame Lenoir at length?
4. When does Paul say he will phone again?

Conversation 3   At the Customs desk
1. What is the age of the traveller, and what is his/her home town?
2. What two other articles does the traveller say s/he has bought, when s/he mentions the souvenirs?
3. Where did s/he buy the watch, and on what date?
4. How much did it cost?
5. What news does the Customs officer then give to the traveller?

Conversation 4   At an exchange bureau or bank
1. Why is the traveller looking for an exchange bureau?
2. What is *not* necessary, and what *is* necessary?
3. How much money will s/he receive altogether?
4. Where must s/he go next?
5. How much money does s/he want in 50-franc notes?

LESSON 7
At a cafe or restaurant

Conversation 1   Ordering sandwiches
1. What sorts of sandwiches are on offer?
2. What does Madame Lebrun choose?
3. What does Nicolas choose?
4. What does Louise choose?
5. What does M. Lebrun order besides the sandwiches?

Conversation 2   Ordering the main meal
1. What are M. Lebrun's first two requests to the waiter?
2. What is the price of the set meal he orders?
3 to 5 Name in order the three starters chosen.
6 to 8 Name in order the three main courses chosen.
9. What do they order to drink?

Conversation 3   Checking the bill
1. Which sort of menu had the family chosen?
2. What is the total cost of the meal apart from the coffee?
3. What had they *not* ordered, and what charge had been made for this?
4. What other charge had been added?
5. Why does M. Lebrun forgive the waiter?

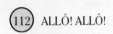

LESSON 8
Lost property and repairs

Conversation 1   At the lost property office
1 What has the visitor lost?
2 When and where was it lost?
3 What was in it?
4 Describe it.
5 What is the visitor told to do?

LESSON 9
Asking for information

Conversation 1   At the information bureau
1 Where is the information bureau situated?
1 When the visitor asks for a list of hotels, what is s/he also given?
2 S/he also receives some leaflets. What are these about?
3 What place does the visitor want to go to, and what instructions are given for reaching

LESSON 10
Illness and accidents

Conversation 1   A road accident
1–3 What three injuries have been caused by the accident?
4 What does the other driver want to find?
5 What two things does the driver give to help the injured people?
6 What hopeful news does the driver give them?
7 What does the driver offer to help with making a report?

Conversation 2   Making an appointment
1 What is the caller's first question?
2 What time does the dentist hold his surgery?
3 What is wrong with the caller?
4 What special offer does the receptionist make to help the caller?
5 What two further questions does the receptionist ask?

LESSON 11
House and home

Conversation 1   Arriving at your penfriend's house
1 What is the first question put to the visitor?
2 Why does the host(ess) say that the guest is very kind?
3 What does the visitor ask if s/he may do?
4 What three things does the visitor need?
5 Write in French one of the two answers the host(ess) gives when the visitor says than

Conversation 2   Discussing daily routine
1 What time does the guest usually go to bed and get up?
2 At what time does the guest have breakfast, lunch and evening meal at home?
3 What does s/he do at four o'clock?
4 In what three ways does the guest help with the housework at home?
5 What sort of help would the host(ess) like?

Conversation 3   Introducing some one
1 Who is Mark?
2 When did he arrive, and how long is he staying?
3 Whereabouts in England does Mark live?
4 What was Jean's opinion of Mark's home town?
5 What is Marie's telephone number?

LESSON 12
Places of entertainment

Conversation 1   Going to the cinema
1 In what part of the cinema are the friends going to sit?
2 What is the cost of two seats?
3 How do the two friends plan to fill in the time till the show begins (two details)?
4 Give the French for (*a*) comedies (*b*) cowboy films (*c*) gangster films
5 Give two details about the film they are going to see.

LESSON 13
At a garage or petrol station

Conversation 1   At the petrol station
1 How much petrol does the driver want?
2 How much does (*a*) the top-grade petrol (*b*) the standard petrol cost?
3 What else does the driver wish to buy?
4 Which places are (*a*) a long way away? (*b*) 20 km, away? (*c*) 2 km, away?
5 Where can sweets and drinks be bought?